Ghosts
of Cornwall

PETER UNDERWOOD

President of
The Ghost Club Society

Bossiney Books · Launceston

FOR

Air Commodore R Carter Jonas
of Fowey

in friendship

This reprint 2010
This edition published 1998 by Bossiney Books Ltd
Langore, Launceston, Cornwall PL15 8LD

ISBN 978-1-89938310-8

Acknowledgements

The photographs are reproduced by kind permission as follows: The Ghost
Club Society Collection, pages 42 and 90; Royal Institution of Cornwall,
pages 6, 41 and 99; Peter Underwood, pages 33, 35, 66 and 93; David Wood,
page 76. Other photographs from the publisher's own collection.

All the line illustrations are by Peter Honeywill.

Printed in Great Britain by R Booth Ltd, Penryn, Cornwall

About the Author

Peter Underwood FRSA is Life President of that famous investigating organisation, The Ghost Club Society, and he must have heard more first-hand ghost stories than any other person alive.

A long-standing member of The Society for Psychical Research, Vice-President of the Unitarian Society for Psychical Studies, a member of The Folklore Society, The Dracula Society and a former member of the Research Committee of the Psychic Research Organisation, he has lectured, written and broadcast extensively. He took part in the first official investigation into a haunting, and has sat with physical and mental mediums, and conducted investigations at seances. He has also been present at exorcisms and experiments with dowsing, precognition, clairvoyance, hypnotism, and regression. He has conducted worldwide tests in telepathy and extra-sensory perception, and has personally investigated scores of haunted houses.

He possesses comprehensive files of alleged hauntings in every county of the British Isles as well as in many foreign countries, and his knowledge and experience have resulted in his being interviewed and consulted on psychic and occult matters by such organisations as the BBC and ITV.

He is a former Honorary Librarian of the London Savage Club, 1 Whitehall Place, London SW1A 2HD, where he can be contacted.

Introduction

Cornwall is a land of mystery where, even today, in some hamlets and away from the busy roads, there is an atmosphere not altogether of this world. Once over the strangely winding Tamar and into Cornwall the visitor enters a mystic land, and it is indisputable that visits to this Celtic county leave an indelible impression on the mind. Those who are lucky enough to return again and again never really escape from the enchantment of the place – or want to.

Cornwall is full of ghosts. There are strange stories of diminutive figures, of silent and brooding forms, of invisible influences, of repeated appearances, of haunted houses and ghostly cities; it is a rich hunting ground for the ghost seeker and for those who appreciate the odd, the miraculous and the inexplicable. The ghosts of Cornwall are a varied bunch indeed and if the browsing of their stories gives as much pleasure to the reader as the research and recounting gave to the author he will be more than satisfied.

While compiling this book, I have met some fascinating people and heard some remarkable stories. For the sake of completeness, I have included, briefly, most of the better-known ghost stories, but I hope I have said something fresh about each of these accounts. In the main, however, I have tried to find new and little-known stories of ghostly encounters.

And, needless to say, I am still looking for genuine ghost stories, everywhere, but especially in beautiful Cornwall.

Peter Underwood

The Savage Club
1 Whitehall Place
London SW1A 2HD

Bedruthan

You catch your breath when you see Bedruthan Steps for the first time, and thousands of people every year visit the sixty acres of spectacular clifftop scenery overlooking the beach and countless miles of ocean. But it has been claimed this was once the site of tin and iron mines and a very ancient castle. Here the slurred and weary tread of long-dead miners in their heavy boots and the 'click-click' of their picks have long been reported by quiet visitors who have no knowledge of the area.

In 1981 I met a local man who had heard the clicking sounds many times, sounds that he and others accept as paranormal, although the sceptical say they are caused by underground water. No such explanation is possible, however, for the grey forms that have been seen here at night, disappearing where no human form could go. Such a form was reported to me in the summer of 1996.

Bodmin

The atmospheric two hundred year old Bodmin Gaol is haunted by the sounds of rattling keys and heavy footsteps, by unexplained voices and vague forms, and by an overwhelming feeling of depression and utter despondency, all seemingly dating from the days when public hangings regularly took place at this doleful place. Much of the building is little changed and memories of the misery experienced here lingers in the expectant air.

Lanhydrock House, near Bodmin, has the gentle ghost of a little old lady. Dressed in grey or possibly black, she haunts the Gallery and the Drawing Room, the oldest parts of this lovely house and the area which escaped the disastrous fire of 1881.

The Grey Lady, as she is known, has been seen walking down the Gallery, the great room of the house running the length of the north wing. She is also often seen sitting on one of the gilded beechwood armchairs in the Drawing Room and is at first taken to be a real person; but as soon as she is approached, the figure disappears. Nobody knows her identity; it has been suggested she is Isabella, the second wife of John, 2nd Baron Robartes (1608-1685). The Robartes family owned Lanhydrock from 1620 until the property passed to the National Trust in 1953.

The 'female presence' that has been distinctly felt on occasions in Her Ladyship's Room would appear to be a different visitor from the past; possibly the Lady Robartes who, at the age of sixty-eight, was rescued by means of a ladder from an upstairs window at the time the house was virtually gutted by fire, but who died a few days later, never having recovered from the shock. Her husband could not get over the tragic loss of his wife and his home, and he died the following year.

During the course of a number of visits to Lanhydrock, the then Assistant Administrator, Tim Belton, told me that on several occasions the odour of fresh cigar smoke had been noticed appropriately enough in the vicinity of the Smoking Room on the ground floor; a smell that was quite unmistakable and completely inexplicable. Possibly some psychic echo from the past.

Bolventor

Isolated and romantic, high up on Bodmin Moor, stands Jamaica Inn, immortalised by Dame Daphne du Maurier when she used it as the setting for her well-known novel of smuggling days, which was later filmed under the same name.

Unexplained footsteps, believed to be those of a young man who was murdered at the inn, are said to echo round the stone floors at regular times of the year, and mysterious hoofbeats have been reported on certain nights. During the month of August, a few years ago, the midnight hoofbeats were said to have been heard repeatedly. Sometimes, too, especially on foggy nights, the figure of a man on horseback has been seen waiting outside. The old coach road which runs from Launceston to Bodmin was once the haunt of smugglers and highwaymen, and, although the road, changed and improved over the years, now bypasses Bolventor, the inn itself has not altered greatly in the last hundred years.

My wife and I used to look in at Jamaica Inn from time to time, remembering earlier visits when we parked our car in the cobbled courtyard, over which stagecoaches used to rattle. The inn sign swings and creaks above in the breeze as we make our way through the great wooden door beneath the porch leading into the lounge, a large stone-flagged room containing a wonderful collection of swords, muskets, lanterns and old brass hanging from the ceiling. In one corner a doorway leads into Mary's Bar, named after Mary Yellan, the heroine of Daphne du Maurier's story. It is at this bar, many years ago, that a stranger stood drinking a pot of ale he was fated never to finish, for, upon being called outside, he put his half-empty tankard on the bar and disappeared into the night.

In the morning his murdered body was found out on the moor, but the identity of his assailant has never been discovered. More than one landlord has heard ghostly footsteps tramping along the passage to the bar – are they those of the murdered man returning to finish his drink?

Some years ago there was a great deal of correspondence in *Country Life* about a strange man who was often seen by many people sitting on the wall outside the inn. He never spoke or moved and his description seemed, from everyone's account, to have been so similar to that of the murdered stranger that it was thought he must be the dead man's ghost.

Jamaica Inn certainly has a brooding atmosphere. It is reputed to be over five hundred years old and still contains some of the original walls of local granite, in places six feet (nearly two metres) thick: is it possible for past events to impregnate these old stones that must have seen smugglers and wreckers in past days?

A few years ago a couple reported seeing a ghost in their bedroom when they spent one night at the inn. Shortly after falling asleep they awoke to see a man standing by the bedroom door, the last room on the right in the upstairs corridor. He seemed to be wearing a three-cornered hat and a long, old-fashioned, tight-waisted overcoat. As they watched, he slowly moved past the end of the bed and disappeared through a large wardrobe. Both witnesses said the room was icy cold while the figure was visible. Next morning, when they related their experience to the landlord, he did not seem in the least surprised and merely said: 'The old boy always goes through the wardrobe when he returns to that room.'

Boscastle

The fascinating Wellington Hotel, a sixteenth-century coaching inn which my wife and I visited regularly for years, has been the scene of a number of ghost sightings and mysterious disturbances.

Soon after Solange and Victor Tobutt bought the 'Welly' in 1986, Victor looked up the stairs to the landing one day and saw to his surprise a frock-coated figure move across the landing. The ruffled shirt, ponytail and leather gaiters suggested a coachman or stable lad.

Going down to the bar where head barman Tom Gregory was standing, Victor began to describe what he had seen when Tom interrupted him with an exact description of the figure. Tom, who had worked at the Welly for about twenty years, said the ghostly figure had been sighted on several occasions.

There have also been sightings of a man who committed suicide and of a young girl, said to have been crossed in love, on the landing at the top of the tower. The ghostly girl was seen by Bill Searle, a retired police officer. She appeared to be completely solid and natural, but emerged out of a wall and disappeared through a closed window.

Eighteen months later he saw her again in the same place, but by this time a flat had been built in the adjoining attic and where there had been a window there was now a door; the girl disappeared through the closed door.

Rooms 9 and 10 at the back of the hotel have been the scene of unexplained happenings as well. Some of the staff have felt a distinct presence in room 10, and on one occasion Bill Searle encountered a little old lady sitting on the bed. Staff member Debbie Jordan was checking these rooms one day when she saw an old lady go through the door of room 9, which she understood to be vacant. She reported back to the receptionist, Jackie Yates, who confirmed the room was indeed vacant, and they decided to visit it together. It was empty when they checked, but then Debbie realised the old lady had gone through the door and had not opened it. It sounded like the same ghost seen by Bill Searle in room 10.

In February 1996 a visitor who was interested in the supernatural asked one of the receptionists, Sandra Winstanley, whether he might walk along the passage leading to rooms 9 and 10. He returned to report that 'the little old lady in room 10 is grateful that when Sandra visited the room at 2.30 p.m. she did not spend long there and did not disturb her'. He also said the ghost was a friendly one. Sandra could not believe her ears, as 2.30 p.m. was when she would normally check the rooms whilst housekeeping, and she always made sure her time in room 10 was kept to a minimum!

Stopping at the Welly in July 1996 my wife and I passed the doorway to the old part of the building and made our way up the final set of stairs to our room, number 17. There my wife mentioned, quite casually, that there must be some sort of celebration going on judging from the decorations she had noticed as we passed the open doorway. I said I hadn't seen any decorations and I popped down to look. There were none, a fact my wife immediately confirmed, much to her surprise.

That night, my wife found herself suddenly wide awake and aware that someone was standing beside the bed, close to her. It was not in the least frightening, but she overwhelmingly felt that someone, probably a man, was standing there. She saw nothing, however, and thought about waking me but, realising I was fast asleep and there was nothing to see, she decided not to disturb me. After a little while, the 'impression' disappeared and she went back to sleep.

At the top of Penally Hill, nestling among trees overlooking lonely Boscastle Harbour, stands haunted Penally House. Built by a local wines and spirits merchant, William Sloggatt, in 1836, it originally had seventeen rooms. Local people suspected Sloggatt was involved in smuggling and that he used the house as a secret storehouse. Subsequently the house passed through many hands and Carolyn Dymond, who was born at Penally House, has revealed it is haunted.

The ghost is thought to be that of a previous owner, Colonel Hawker. There have been reports of mysterious footsteps being heard both inside and outside the house.

Miss Frances Baxter, who bought the house in 1954, was in

her bedroom one afternoon when she distinctly saw someone pass the window. She waited for the person to pass the other window, but nobody did. She immediately went outside, but no one was in sight; she made extensive enquiries and established to her satisfaction that no living person had passed her window and been seen by her – perhaps it was a psychic echo from past smuggling days.

Penally House has played a large part in the history of Boscastle and there are continuing stories of underground tunnels, secret shafts and inexplicable footsteps and hoofbeats on the private road that Sloggatt cut out of the rock from the house to the harbour. Sloggatt's three sons were transported to Australia for smuggling.

Bossiney

A first-hand account of a haunted farmhouse in Bossiney is to be found in *The Folklore of Cornwall*. Here I paraphrase the salient points.

The informant was about eleven years of age when she and her sister stayed with their parents at the house, said to be one of the oldest buildings in the Bossiney area. One morning the two girls awoke to find that some large and heavy framed paintings had been removed from the wall in the night and now stood with their backs to the room, on the floor. The informant's mother and another guest examined the pictures at the time and agreed that neither of the children could have been responsible: the paintings were simply too heavy.

A few nights later the informant's father, who was sleeping in an adjoining room, was awakened by the rattle of a pitcher and bowl which stood on the deep window ledge in the room occupied by the children. On entering the room he found the informant sitting cross-legged on the ledge, apparently staring out to sea. When he asked her what she was doing she said she had seen a little, bent old man, who had whispered to her and she could not remember anything else.

Next day the owner of the house was asked whether she had

been disturbed by the noise during the night. She wanted to know exactly what had happened and afterwards said she hadn't said anything earlier in case they wouldn't stay in the room, but that part of the house was supposed to be haunted by the ghost of a hunchback who had lived there and he was in the habit of sitting at the window in question, cross-legged and staring out to sea.

The family stayed at the farmhouse for three years running. On one occasion the mother and one of the daughters had gone into Launceston with some friends, leaving the informant, who suffered with car-sickness, with her father. The weather was dull and miserable, and in the afternoon, feeling thoroughly fed-up, the girl went upstairs to her bedroom and there saw an old man sitting hunched-up in a cross-legged position on the window ledge. For the rest of their visit she had terrifying dreams and a very real fear of the haunted bedroom. She was totally unaware of the fact that it was supposed to be haunted until some years later.

Nearby, St Nectan's Glen has a strange and indescribable air of unreality. It has been called 'one of the most beautiful corners of North Cornwall' by local man Michael Williams who has chronicled the experiences of several people living in the area: a writer, who lived nearby, claimed he had often heard the sound of chanting monks at night; another local man said he had heard the sounds of sobbing and weird laughter; and Kathleen Everard talked of beautiful organ music emanating from an empty building...

Saint Nectan who, after being decapitated, is credited with picking up his head, is reported to have appeared at Hartland Church in Devon. There are also stories of the saint warning sailors of submerged rocks by ringing a silver bell from his tower. From the lane by the former Rocky Valley Hotel, you can follow a path which takes you on the route which pilgrims trod in the sixth century when they went to pray at the shrine of St Nectan. Today the hermitage and the whole glen that bears the saint's name are haunted places.

On several occasions when we were there, both my wife and I thought the atmosphere overwhelmingly expectant, and it was easy to accept the stories of strange figures appearing and vanishing inexplicably; of cats and dogs being worried and acting strangely for no apparent reason; of snatches of music, footsteps, whispering and chanting. In particular we were told about a hooded figure in a grey habit with a blue lining to the hood, very kindly-looking but somehow troubled, and I like to think that on occasions this troubled saint returns to the place he loved – perhaps to ascertain the whereabouts of the treasure reputedly buried with him and his sacramental vessels somewhere in the bed of the river at this idyllic spot.

Botathan near Launceston

A curious story was told by the Reverend John Ruddle; a story, seemingly, of a spirit earthbound by an unconfessed sin.

A young woman named Dorothy Dinglet (or Dingle) died here and although little is known of her life and loves, a family named Bligh could be best described as acquaintances of the dead woman, no more.

There were two sons in the Bligh household, one a young man, the other a schoolboy. Almost immediately after Dorothy Dinglet's death the elder son left the area and is heard of no more; it is not known whether there is any connection between the two events, although there are suggestions that Dorothy died in childbirth, the father being the elder Bligh brother.

About three years later the younger boy, who crossed a certain field on his way to school each day, was troubled by a ghostly form he met each morning.

The form was that of a young woman who walked towards him, pointing to something in the distance. He recognised her as Dorothy Dinglet, but she took no notice of him, just steadily gliding over the grass and passing out of his vision on the opposite side of the field.

The constant sighting of the visionary figure began to unnerve the boy, so his father approached the Reverend John Ruddle, then curate at Launceston. The priest heard the boy's story and readily agreed to accompany him next morning on his way through the field. Much to his astonishment he, too, clearly saw the figure, and he prepared himself to speak to it but was overcome with fear until the figure had passed.

Ruddle then asked permission from his Bishop to exorcise the ghost and, leave being at length granted, he went alone to the field where he was prepared to wrestle with the earthbound spirit he was convinced he was dealing with.

His preparations indicated a somewhat curious and certainly deep knowledge of matters not usually known to country clergymen: he carried a crutch of rowan; he traced a circle on the grass and drew a pentacle within the circle, setting his rowan stick at the point where the five angles intersected; and, facing north, he waited for the ghost to appear.

When the phantom form duly put in an appearance John Ruddle read aloud from a parchment commands which he repeated three times and then he addressed the ghost in Syriac, a language, he said, 'which is used where such ones dwell and converse in thoughts that glide.'

He then induced the ghost to enter the circle and gently asked her why she was not at rest. She replied that it was because she had committed a certain sin in life; she confessed the sin and the priest 'released her troubled spirit'. The following morning, according to John Ruddle, he met her again and after certain commands she disappeared towards the west and was not seen again; but evidence in my possession suggests the ghost of Dorothy Dinglet was seen subsequently on a number of occasions and there are those who believe her unquiet spirit still walks on misty mornings.

The exorcism of the ghost of Dorothy Dinglet is supposed to have taken place in a field called Higher Brown Quartils and for years there was a path running through the field that was known as 'Dorothy Dinglet's Path.'

Camborne

After one of my broadcasts about ghosts and haunted houses, Mrs M A King of Camborne wrote telling me about a curious experience she had one fine Easter Monday. I do not think I can do better than quote from that original letter and the subsequent correspondence:

'I take the dog for walks along the country roads not far from here and on this occasion, as we were climbing a long and steep hill, I noticed a woman some 20 yards or so [nearly 20 metres] further up the hill, about to mount a bicycle. As we were both on the same side of the road (a busy one, I might add), it was obvious that she would be passing quite close to me in a minute or so. Unfortunately, in the split second that I looked down at the dog and then raised my eyes again, she had completely vanished – bicycle and all.

'The road was especially steep at the place where she had been and it was very wide too. If she had changed her mind and gone back the way she had come, she would have had to cross the road, turn the bicycle round and begin pushing it up the hill. The only alternative to this would have been for her to cross a rather wide grass verge and go through into a field; but there was no gate at that particular spot and the hedges were very high. In either of these events I would have been bound to see her.

'I often try to recall what she looked like and as far as I can remember she was about thirty-five or forty years old, slight with a sallow complexion, poorly dressed in a grey cardigan and I think she was wearing a hat.

'As near as I can remember the time would be between half past three and four o'clock. The place was a continuation of Tehidy Road, which runs alongside the Red River and joins the main road somewhere close to Tehidy Hospital.'

As Mrs King says in a subsequent letter, it would be interesting to know whether a person answering such a description had been killed on the road at that point and particularly whether other people have seen a female cyclist who disappeared near Camborne.

Camelford

The ghost of part of a knight has been seen at a Queen Anne house overlooking the square. One night a previous occupant had found herself suddenly wide awake in the middle of the night and she saw the clear figure of a knight standing by her bed. He appeared to be quite solid and normal in every way except that his body ended at the knees, which appeared to rest

on the floor. Subsequent enquiries established that the house, which has traces of Tudor cellars and walls, has been altered many times over the years. The floor level in the room where the ghost was seen had, in fact, been raised, suggesting that the phantom knight was appearing exactly where it had always appeared. I wonder whether anyone who happened to be in the room below would have seen a pair of metal-clad legs sticking out of the ceiling! I understand that the figure was readily visible by virtue of the fact that a bright moon shone into the room through the window.

Nearby Slaughter Bridge, traditionally the scene of King Arthur's last battle, has a strange atmosphere to this day. Upstream from the bridge, on a bank close to the water, an oblong slab of moss-covered granite is regarded by some as King Arthur's Gravestone.

Experts are divided on whether in 537 the Battle of Camlann, in which Arthur and Mordred fell, took place here, but some bloody battle must have been fought for it to be perpetuated in the name of the bridge. Perhaps it has something to do with the misty and unexplained figures that have been seen occasionally crossing the bridge and disappearing into the history-laden air which surrounds this strange place.

Incidentally, after his death King Arthur's spirit is said to have entered a chough (the red-legged Cornish crow) at Slaughter Bridge and bad luck was said to come to anyone who killed this bird.

Cotehele

Cotehele House near Calstock belonged to the Edgcumbe family from 1353 until it was acquired by the National Trust in 1947. In 1553, however, the family moved eleven miles away to Mount Edgcumbe, and from then onwards the house was only occupied occasionally. It therefore escaped major alteration, enlargement or rebuilding, and the parts open to visitors are much as they were more than three hundred years ago. The furnishings of the house have also remained largely undisturbed, providing perhaps an ideal setting and environment for ghostly perambulations.

Yet beautiful Cotehele is usually free of ghostly manifestations apart from the occasional powerful whiff of perfume that has repeatedly been reported by visitors and many members of the staff, in the east wing and elsewhere. The Administrator and others at the house tell me the odour is suggestive of a herbal fragrance and is, so far, quite inexplicable.

At least one visitor, totally unaware that such a fragrance had been repeatedly experienced before, reported an overwhelming odour of herbal fragrance accompanied by 'plaintive music' in the oldest part of the house.

Of course there are legends associated with Cotehele. One story goes that in some long-forgotten quarrel in the dim and distant past a man was killed beneath the archway leading to the present entrance at Cotehele, and the spot where he fell and expired remained forever marked by an irremovable bloodstain. Small wonder then that there are vague stories, too, of a ghostly form being seen hereabouts seemingly, from the costume, dating back to the seventeenth century.

The 'bloodstained' stone was moved to the little bridge by ancient Cotehele Quay and painted over, thereby obscuring a curiosity and perhaps placating a ghostly manifestation. The presence of red ironstone in the area must suggest that the so-called 'bloodstained' stone was in all probability a particularly vivid natural display of the veins in the stone which can look very much like blood when it is wet.

Mrs Phyllis Julyan resided for very many years at Cotehele and she told me that for her the old house always had a lovely atmosphere. While she was not able to feel or see ghosts, she believed completely that the people who once lived there were happy and contented individuals. Nevertheless she was good enough to relate two ghostly episodes.

The first occurred during the last illness of the 5th Earl of Mount Edgcumbe when a nurse from Tavistock was sitting by his bedside. She noticed a woman dressed in white pass through the room and, since at that time anyone could walk right round the house through the various rooms surrounding the courtyard, she took no notice, thinking it must be the housekeeper. Later she encountered the housekeeper and, noticing she was dressed in black, the nurse said to her: 'Have you changed your dress because when you passed through the Earl's room surely you were wearing a white dress?' The housekeeper told her she had certainly not changed her dress and furthermore she had not been near the Earl's room that morning. She also added: 'You must have seen the ghost...'

Another more personal experience befell Mrs Julyan at Christmas, 1980, when a friend telephoned her after calling to wish her the compliments of the season. On the telephone this friend asked Mrs Julyan whether a young girl was staying with her, a girl with long hair and wearing a white, flowing dress; for she had encountered such a figure going down the private staircase as she had left Mrs Julyan. No such person was in fact staying at the house and no one of that description was ever traced.

In such a lovely old house as Cotehele it must seem likely that ghostly emanations from the past still linger and are occasionally visible or sensed in some way by people who are sensitive to such things.

Crafthole

The beach at Whitsand Bay was the scene of many a smuggled cargo and the well-known freetrader who had headed a gang of like-minded men was named Finny. Their headquarters was a public house on the Torpoint to Looe road, then known as the New Inn.

One night Finny's luck ran out. He and his followers were surprised by revenue men and in the resulting short but sharp skirmish Finny was killed.

Thereafter his ghost was reported to frequently revisit the scene of his earthly triumphs and final desperate struggle, and in 1950 the brewers, I am told, renamed the inn in honour of their ghost. Today the old New Inn has become The Finnygook Inn.

Forrabury

Ghostly bells with ghostly chimes have long been associated with the waters here. It seems that new bells for the local church were conveyed by a blasphemous sea captain who, on arrival, forgot the sacred nature of his cargo to the extent that he cursed the elements for his tempestuous journey – whereupon a violent storm broke and mountainous waves rolled over the vessel and it sank, with all hands, in sight of the village inhabitants.

As it foundered, the bells in the ship's hold rang for the first and last time for the people of Forrabury; except that whenever a storm is brewing in the area a peal of phantom bells reportedly echoes from beneath the waves, and to this day no bells hang in the belfry of the local church. I have talked with people who have not only heard the ghost bells but have also allegedly seen phantom boats with phantom crews rowing silently to the spot where the ship sank. In 1996 I myself, together with my springer spaniel, heard an echoing bell tolling from the direction of the sea at haunted Forrabury.

Gulval

Following my broadcast entitled 'Strange to Relate' concerning a phantom motor vehicle, Mrs Marion Grace Paul wrote to me from St Ives and subsequently was good enough to supply me with full details relating to a haunted house at Gulval.

In the late 1950s Mrs Paul and her husband were house-hunting and they became interested in a large corner house that was for sale. One sunny afternoon they set out to see over the house. While waiting for someone to show them round the property Mrs Paul went down a few steps on the ground floor and was looking out of a window, one hand on the windowsill, when she suddenly had an overwhelming feeling that the place had a very evil atmosphere. She knew immediately it would not be a good place to live. Furthermore this unexpected impression of the house was accompanied by an intense shock or charge that seemed to travel up her arm from the hand on the windowsill: a powerful shock that left her arm feeling paralysed. They soon left the house and went to Penzance to call on Mrs Paul's parents to see whether they could find out anything about the history of the house. Mrs Coulson Paul, a Penzance person by birth, said immediately in reply to their enquiry: 'Oh, didn't you know a woman was murdered there?'

Shortly afterwards Mr and Mrs Paul, still intrigued by the atmosphere inside the house at Gulval, related their experience to a long-standing friend who lived at Mousehole. He remembered that a friend of his, who had been looking for accommodation, had obtained a room there at the top of the house. One evening, Mrs Paul's friend told them, he had gone to visit his friend and as he opened the downstairs front door a small black dog had slipped inside and run up the stairs ahead of him and disappeared into a room where the door stood open. Feeling responsible for letting the dog into the house, he thought he should find it and put it outside again, but there was no sign of the dog in the empty room where he had seen it enter seconds earlier and there appeared to be no place whatever where it could be concealed.

He now became aware of a very curious atmosphere; when he eventually located his friend, who seemed obsessed with the house and would not hear a word against it, he nevertheless advised him to move as soon as possible for his own good.

Shortly afterwards this friend who resided in the haunted house was returning home one night when he apparently saw a car coming straight towards him; he swerved to avoid it but in so doing drove into the path of another car and was killed in the ensuing crash. His companion in the car described the 'phantom' vehicle to the police. Other witnesses said the car swerved as if to avoid something they could not see and so ran into the other car, with fatal results.

A resident of Marazion has revealed that efforts were made to exorcise the house at one time, following repeated appearances of a ghostly 'white lady' seen leaving the house, crossing the road and making her way to the beach where, it was said, she had committed suicide.

A man who now lives in Sussex visited the house to call on a friend and encountered a lady in old-fashioned riding habit, standing at the top of the stairs – a figure that vanished inexplicably. Another witness saw a small black dog which disappeared when she tried to touch it.

I may say that I have the names and addresses of all the people concerned in these experiences, but out of respect for their privacy I am not revealing any further details. I am hoping, however, to conduct an investigation at the house in the not too distant future.

Gwithian

Nearby Hell's Mouth, where there are cliffs nearly 275 feet (85 metres) high, is reputed to be haunted by the sounds of a suicide's cries.

Many and varied are the tales told and written about The Mouth of Hell, but the haunting appears to correspond with the story of a black-hearted rogue who threw himself headlong into the angry waters at the foot of the towering Black Cliffs.

It was wild country hereabouts in days gone by and not a few of the tunnels that run underground at the foot of the cliffs at Hell's Mouth were useful for hiding smuggled goods of one kind or another. A freetrader, whose descendants still live in Cornwall, lived in a nearby valley with his sister, and he and a boon companion prospered from the proceeds of a nefarious life until his friend was suddenly arrested. He was hurriedly taken under escort to Launceston, where he would certainly have been hanged, but neither the prisoner nor the escort arrived at Launceston. News travelled fast among the freetraders and the two men thought it wise to set their backs on Cornwall for a while.

The freetrader's sister was as gentle as he was wild and he loved her more than life itself, but she knew that he had to leave the country. Amid tears he set off, promising to return one day.

Some time later, raiders came ashore under cover of a threatening storm, pillaging the countryside, firing the villages and homesteads and taking away the cattle and the people they had not slaughtered.

When the freetrader returned he found only smouldering ruins where once his home had stood and the ravaged body of his murdered sister. Driven to distraction by the loss of the one person he loved so dearly, he hurried to the high cliffs to see whether there was any trace of the murdering raiders, but they had all gone. As he stood with the roaring sea at his feet and the sound of seagulls in his ears, he became overwhelmed with despair and threw himself over what is now called Hell's Mouth. And ever since it is said that when the wind is in the north-west and heavy seas are rolling in from the coast of Labrador, as they were that night long, long ago, then the cries of the broken-hearted freetrader echo again among these ageless rocks.

A few years ago some mining students camped upon the rocks below Hell's Mouth and afterwards they said they had heard fierce yells and snatches of old sea shanties echoing from the caves and tunnels beneath the Mouth of Hell.

Heligan

The Lost Gardens of Heligan, north of Mevagissey, have a magic all their own. People have lived at Heligan since prehistoric times, and from time to time something intangible from those far off days seems to return to this atmospheric place. There is often a deathly stillness in the Lost Valley where unexplained forms of primitive life have been glimpsed. In the Old Wood, in particular, there is sometimes a complete absence of bird song; on other occasions bird song of an overwhelming and varied quality fills the air.

Tim Smit, author of the excellent *Lost Gardens of Heligan*, told me in September 1997 that 'there have been many strange experiences at Heligan ... which have been relayed to me by those I trust.' During the course of his book Tim relates stories he heard of the Grey Lady 'who is said to be regularly seen walking away from the house. In fact, that part of the ride between the house and the shelter belt woodlands is often referred to on old maps as Grey Lady's Walk.' An elderly lady resident of Mevagissey told Tim she had once seen the apparition and followed it into the trees where it disappeared.

A number of visitors have claimed to see 'someone' walking through the wall of the Crystal Grotto; there are innumerable instances of visitors being aware they were 'not alone' in the area of the Wishing Well and adjacent Rockery. Even those who know the gardens have had odd experiences, such as enormous black shapes suddenly appearing and slowly drifting away, and on occasions dogs have shown every indication of seeing something invisible to their human companions. There have even been visits by clergymen who have attempted to cleanse the atmosphere.

I have talked with workers who won't go in certain parts of the garden at certain times of the day – or night – and one local gardener told me he never goes near the place without a quiver of uneasy fear passing through him, although he has nothing but praise for the wonderful place and the remarkable success that is The Lost Gardens of Heligan.

Helston

Nearby Godolphin House, the former home of the Earls of Godolphin, is reputedly haunted by Margaret Godolphin, according to an article in the *Western Morning News* and several other published sources.

The house was the home of the Godolphin family for centuries and the ghost of the unhappy Margaret, who died in childbirth in 1678, is alleged to have been sighted on numerous occasions. These were usually in the vicinity of the entrance hall of the house, where she was seen to emerge from a tiny closet, long since sealed up, and move out onto the terrace and into the avenue of old trees and there 'to walk disconsolately among the shadows'. The body of Margaret Godolphin is buried in the church at Breage.

The eminent historian, Dr A L Rowse, once spent a night at Godolphin sleeping in the guest room, perhaps within an arm's length of the sealed closet, and in an Elizabethan bed, too. He had scarcely fallen asleep before he was awakened by 'the unmistakable swish of a woman's silk dress' sweeping through his bedroom!

The house, which dates back to Tudor times, is said to have

five escape routes that were designed for the safety of Charles II; today the names of the King's Room and the King's Garden remind us of those turbulent times.

Antony Hippisley Coxe told me that nearby Jew's Lane is haunted by the ghost of a Jew who hanged himself from a tree and was buried beneath the road. A ghost bull has long been associated with the area as well, although why this should be so nobody seems to know.

The Beehive Inn, Coinagehall Street, is thought to be haunted by the ghost of a young man who was murdered there over a hundred years ago. The fact that some witnesses have described the figure as being dressed in 'modern style' need not necessarily rule out the murder victim: some suits of a hundred and fifty years ago are strikingly similar to those worn by some young people today and in any case most witnesses of this apparition, which is usually seen an hour or so before midnight, say the form is 'rather shadowy'.

Ladock near Truro

In the valley of the Tresillian River nestles the haunted church of St Ladoca. Nearby, Tresillian Bridge was the scene of the final surrender of the Royalists to Parliamentary forces in 1646 and here the terms of peace were arranged.

The restored Early English church with its Norman font and monuments seems peaceful enough to the casual visitor, but at certain times and especially, I am told, at mid-evening, various people on separate occasions have thought that another person entered the church with them, only to find they were alone once they were inside. At other times, out of the corner of the eye, a shadowy figure has been seen inside the church; a figure or form that disappears whenever it is approached, dissolving swiftly into nothingness.

Mr A M Hammett, who lived for a long time in the vicinity, told me the regular bell-ringers often thought an additional ringer had joined them during their weekly evening practice, but this proved not to be so. 'Many times,' he explained, 'a large number of people over the years have seen the unidentified ghost figure' and now it is more or less accepted that the ghost comes to listen to the bell-ringing. 'I myself did not think such a thing could happen,' Mr Hammett stated, 'but I have experienced it myself on a number of occasions.'

He said there is no feeling of coldness or atmospheric change when the ghost form is seen and he felt sure it is a benign presence. A legend is beginning to grow in the neighbourhood that the ghost is that of a past church warden or bell-ringer who served there for many years and whose personality returns on still summer evenings to the church he loved when the bell-ringers are making their quiet way to the church they also love in their turn.

Lamorna

The old farmplace of Trewoofe, overlooking lovely Lamorna Valley, has many legends and several ghosts. The present owner, Mrs Margaret Powell, tells me she has never seen a ghost at Trewoofe, although 'perceptive' friends feel them. While the stories of ghosts and unusual happenings are, mostly, stories, nevertheless they are based on historical facts and a good knowledge of the locality. 'As a historian,' says Mrs Powell, 'I know the names of everyone who lived in my house back to 1270 and, while I do not take such stories seriously, it is easy to see how these legends came to be passed on. Trewoofe was a medieval manor house and had its mill (the leat still runs above the house and the site of the millpond can still be seen) – not an unlikely place for two children to drown in the time of the Crusades.' This is a reference to one of the most persistent ghost stories associated with Trewoofe; that the ghosts of two drowned children are seen gathering wild flowers by the banks of the former millpond.

Mrs Powell informs me there is a fogou in the woods below Trewoofe and that she has been told it is situated on a ley-line.

Land's End

Marc Alexander told me a strange story about a lonely cove here that is the haunt of a phantom dog whose bite can kill.

It seems that in the sixteenth century the Emperor of China sent, in the care of one of his daughters, a pair of Pekinese dogs, animals that had been bred as early as the eighth century for the Chinese Imperial family, and owned exclusively by them.

A dog and a bitch made the journey, the bitch travelling in a large ivory chest, and during the voyage she gave birth to puppies: baby Lion Dogs of China. A violent storm off the Cornish coast drove the English ship, carrying the Princess and the dogs across the Channel, towards the cliffs of Land's End. The superstitious crew turned on the foreign girl and blamed her presence for the unexpected storm.

They broke into her cabin and threw the unfortunate girl and her dogs overboard, but not before a sailor had been bitten by one of the terrified dogs.

The body of the Chinese Princess was washed ashore in a cove beside the ivory box, but for some time the local people would not go near the strange girl whom they thought must be a foreign demon. When they did eventually open the box all the dogs were dead except for one which soon expired.

The girl and the dogs were buried in the cove. Meanwhile they heard that the sailor who had been bitten by the dog aboard ship had died, and word soon spread that the lonely grave should be avoided because it was guarded by the ghostly Pekinese dog.

From time to time a local man, braver than the rest, would approach the grave at dead of night and dig for the ivory chest which it was thought might contain treasure. Each time, however, invisible teeth would close upon the man's hands or ankles, and invariably the would-be grave-robber died. Eventually even the bravest treasure-seeker left the haunted cove to its ghost.

The last recorded incident dates from the middle of the 19th century when a boy was playing on the beach and came across a piece of carved ivory hidden in the sand. As he reached for it he felt something bite him, although nothing was visible. On his arm were teeth marks and within a few days the boy was dead.

A few miles south at Hella Point there have been sightings of a pair of phantom lovers. Back in the days of sailing ships Nancy (some versions of the story have her named Polly) and a seaman named William were sweethearts. Nancy's father, a

Porthgwarra farmer, disapproved of the young man and so the couple would meet secretly at a spot that became known as Sweethearts' Cove.

William promised that after one more voyage he would leave the sea. After he had gone, Nancy watched and waited for his return from a spot on Hella Point that became known as Nancy's Garden. But the months went by and there was no news from William and no sign of the return of his ship.

One moonlit night Nancy stood for hours, looking out over the sea, and then she wandered down to the cove and sat on a rock. A neighbour saw the sad-faced girl sitting gazing at the sea and she saw, too, that the tide was fast coming in, but the girl made no move to leave her lonely vigil. Fearing that Nancy might let herself drown in the melancholy of her loneliness, the woman began to climb down towards the cliff to see what she could do. When she arrived on the shore she was surprised to see another figure seated on the rock beside Nancy: had William's ship returned and was this the long-awaited lovers' reunion?

Quietly watching she saw the waves come higher and higher. She screamed and shouted to warn the pair, but the lovers either did not hear or did not wish to heed her call. She saw the waters wash over them and they walked out to sea, their hands entwined and each looking into the other's eyes...

No trace of Nancy was ever found and soon word came that William's ship had foundered on its homeward journey and had sunk with all hands. From time to time there are reports of a ghostly pair of lovers walking hand in hand along the shore at Porthgwarra Cove, figures that vanish inexplicably.

Launceston

Following a radio programme on the fascinating subject of 'Haunted Houses' I received a letter from the late Mrs Denise Buckridge of Dockacre House, Launceston, during the course of which she told me that the five-gabled Elizabethan house, built into the side of a hill and occupied by her family, had an interesting haunting associated with it.

Visiting beautiful Dockacre in the company of my much lamented friend, James Turner, I heard the odd story of the alleged haunting and the even odder story of the moving walking sticks. We explored the fine staircase and heard the story of Nicholas Herle who is said to have shot his wife Elizabeth, accidentally or by design, on this very staircase. It is said that for more than two hundred years a large and irremovable blood-stain was to be seen on the second tread up from the hall. Some years ago the staircase treads were removed and all traces of the 'everlasting bloodstain' were lost, although there are inhabitants of Launceston today who remember seeing it.

Nicholas Herle, a noted barrister of the day and twice Mayor of Launceston, in 1716 and 1721, died in 1728 at Hampstead. Pastel portraits of both Nicholas and his wife Elizabeth in the present dining-room have hung there since before Elizabeth died in somewhat mysterious circumstances in 1714. They comprise part of the property and estate and are sold with the house. Elizabeth's monument in the church of St Mary Magdalene refers to her death 'by starvation or other unlawful means'.

At one time there were secret passages leading from Dockacre House to either the church or the nearby castle, and one identified passage entrance is visible in the cellar.

It is said that Elizabeth went mad, and her husband had her locked away in a small upstairs room and there proceeded to systematically starve her, one of the prescribed cures for madness at the time. Unfortunately, he seems to have overdone the treatment. When she was near to death the frenzied Elizabeth escaped from her room and was almost at the bottom of the stairs on her dash for freedom when her husband accidentally or intentionally shot her dead.

One might have expected her ghost to haunt the house, but it is the ghost of Nicholas Herle that has been seen here, usually in the main hall, notwithstanding the fact that he died more than two hundred miles away; and he is also credited with playing a flute whenever a death is about to occur in the house. I examined the flute which cannot be played by mortal man, since one end has long been blocked-up, and it has been made into a walking stick.

Walking sticks seem to have a strong association with Dockacre House. There is a tradition that every owner of Dockacre hands on to his successor a walking stick to add to the collection housed there. I saw the collection which then numbered thirteen, including the 'flute stick'. The sticks were kept in a sack in the attic and, I was told, they were themselves subject to supernormal interference if they were not kept in a particular order, for with much rattling they would then sort themselves out into the correct sequence. They are an interesting collection and include a sword stick, a cane and a stick with a detachable knob capable of secreting poison.

The Rev. Sabine Baring-Gould lived here at one time and he wrote about the ghost in his novel, *John Herring*, where he has the ghost appear to two of his characters at the front door.

When I was at Dockacre I learned that previous owners of the place have reported pictures falling from the walls without any apparent reason and strange bangs and crashing noises at

The author examining the strange flute stick at Dockacre House

night; tappings and the sound of unexplained footsteps and the inexplicable opening and closing of doors. Today Dockacre is a happy house and untroubled by the flute-playing 'Man in Red' of former days. Yet still something of the old atmosphere remains for some visitors.

Mrs Buckridge told me there have been two rather strange occurrences while they have been there. A woman was visiting Launceston after an interval of fifty years and asked whether she could see the house again, as a relative used to live there. She recounted that on occasions when she went to visit, as a child of about eight years old, she would get as far as the main staircase and would suddenly and for no apparent reason feel ill and faint. After this had happened a couple of times she was taken away and never returned to the house. She knew nothing about the reputed ghost at the time or the allegedly violent death on the main staircase.

The other incident concerned a friend who had brought her sister to the house without telling her anything about the ghost or the legend of the sticks. When this girl, aged about twenty, went upstairs and saw the sticks, she turned very pale and became icy cold and rushed down the stairs and out of the house!

The churchyard at Launceston has long been said to be haunted by a kergrim – a Cornish word for a ghoul: an unpleasant ghost associated with burial places. I am also told that the priory ruins harbour the ghost of an Augustinian, black-cowled monk, last seen in 1996. A similar figure was reportedly seen at the now demolished Walk House by Dr Arthur Budd when he lived there and by a later occupant, a boy who had no knowledge of the figure seen by Dr Budd.

Not far from Launceston, amid the rolling countryside, stands a centuries-old house, once a farmhouse and later a holiday home, but it stands on 'ill-wished' land and has long been regarded as an unlucky and haunted place.

Years ago it is said a man hanged himself in the kitchen in the depth of some forgotten despair, and not so long ago a military man reputedly died there in mysterious and unpleasant circumstances.

My informant, a local person of good standing who has known the house and locality all her life, once had permission to use the telephone when the occupants were away. She accordingly went to the house one evening, but just as she was about to use the telephone she heard heavy and regular footsteps sounding on the ceiling over her head, apparently emanating from the room above. She knew there was no human being up there and she hurriedly left the house and never did make that telephone call!

Some years later, one Christmas, she and her mother were invited to the house for Christmas dinner and at the height of the festivities her mother, sitting next to her at table, turned and said sharply, 'Don't shake my chair, dear'. A moment later my informant's own chair was violently shaken and, although they diligently sought for the cause or reason, they never found any explanation. These are just two of the many odd and never explained incidents that seemed always to be occurring.

Another occupant of the house, who also died there very suddenly and at a young age, had a dog which habitually slept over a barn, some 12 feet (3.5 metres) above ground level and reached by means of some stone steps. Occasionally the dog, a friendly and quiet animal, would visit my informant who lived nearby. One night, around midnight, she and her mother heard something scratching at the door and when they went to see what it was, they found the dog from the big house – but he was shivering and cowering with fright. They let the animal inside and settled it down for the night, but in the morning it simply would not go home. Time and time again it was taken up the drive but halfway along it would stop, dig in its feet and refuse to go any further. So the dog passed into the possession of my friend and it lived a happy life for another six years. It is now buried in the garden, but for the rest of its life it would never go all the way along the drive to the house where it had lived for years, nor would it go near the barn where it had slept all its life until that night when something frightened it almost out of its wits. That night it had gnawed its way out of the barn, jumped some fifteen feet (4.5 metres) to the ground and raced down the drive away from the 'something' which it never forgot.

That very odd house, with a very odd name, crouches expectantly in the lush countryside, seemingly waiting for something to happen.

Linkinhorne

Nearby Rillaton is credited with one of Britain's oldest ghosts: a phantom Druidic priest. Legend has it that he would often be seen by travellers beside an ancient tumulus near Rillaton Manor, offering passers-by a drink from a golden cup – a magic cup that could never be emptied.

One night a weary traveller tried to drain the cup and when he found it was impossible to do so, he became annoyed and

then angry. Throwing the wine into the face of the phantom, he remounted his horse and resumed his journey. Soon afterwards he and his horse were found dead at the bottom of a ravine.

This seems all very legendary and unbelievable, but oddly enough Rillaton Barrow was excavated at the beginning of the last century and the skeleton of a man was unearthed and, beside it, a golden cup. The cup is now preserved in the British Museum.

Looe

A ghostly white hare is reputed to run from Talland to Looe and there vanish at the door of The Jolly Sailor Inn.

The phantom animal is supposed to be connected with a young girl who committed suicide. In an effort to make up for her wickedness, she seeks to help the inhabitants of this ancient port, for the transmogrified form is said only to appear when misfortune is about to strike or some danger threatens the town. The original Ye Olde Jolly Sailor Inn was a white-washed water-side haunt of pirates and smugglers, but the story of the girl who killed herself, the reason she runs to the Jolly Sailor, and why she should appear as a white hare, nobody knows.

Looe Island

There is a story, going back to the 1850s, concerning a lady who, while staying for a holiday at a farm here, was frightened when she encountered the ghostly figure of a tall, aristocratic-looking man with beautiful hands and long fingers. He seemed to be enveloped in a kind of bluish haze, walked across the room and disappeared through the opposite wall.

Later the woman heard that several people who had stayed at the farm had reported seeing blue lights which no one could explain, but she never heard of anyone else who had seen the ghostly figure.

Some years afterwards a skeleton was unearthed on the island and was discovered to be that of a tall man with exceptionally long fingers.

Lostwithiel

Braddock Down saw Cromwell's army suffer a rare defeat on 19 January 1643 and ever since, on the anniversary of that battle, the thunder of horses' hooves have been reported to echo mysteriously about the battle area: a curious cyclic phenomenon that has parallels with Edgehill (23 October 1642) and other battlefields. And, as at Edgehill, there are those who have caught a glimpse of war-weary soldiers, Roundheads and Royalists, disappearing into the wintry gloom.

Ludgvan

Here a tall figure, swathed from head to foot in white, has frightened many people; a figure that always seems to disappear in the vicinity of a churchyard wall.

One witness, a stranger to the area knowing nothing of any reputed ghosts, became lost in the middle of a storm one night. As he decided to make enquiries at the next house, he became aware that he was being followed by a tall and white figure, a form that disconcertingly kept the same distance behind him, no matter whether he slowed down or increased the speed of his pace. After a while the traveller found himself along a churchyard wall, over which he could see wet gravestones gleaming in the moonlight. He looked behind him and saw the figure that had been following him for perhaps ten minutes. Suddenly it turned and disappeared in the direction of the graveyard. Another witness described seeing a hooded figure in the graveyard gateway. Similar stories created something approaching panic among the local people a few years ago and no one would go anywhere near the burial ground after dusk.

Some writers have connected this tall, white form with the publicly-hanged Sarah Polgrain (see the entry for Mount's Bay), but there is really very little evidence to support such a suggestion, especially as reports of a tall, white shape which frequents the churchyard were in circulation before the Sarah Polgrain case.

Marazion

St Michael's Mount, that romantic fortified monastery, has several ancient legends associated with it as well as a bed that no child can sleep in.

The legend includes a one-eyed giant and, appropriately, a vision of St Michael himself, but for more recent psychic manifestations Lord St Levan tells me he can only confirm that a four-poster bedstead, dating from the seventeenth century, has a very curious atmosphere which many people have remarked upon. The bedstead is decorated with figureheads of Spanish

ships that were wrecked off the Cornish coast hereabouts and no child, it seems, has ever been able to spend a night in the bed.

A ghostly 'white lady' has long been said to haunt the vicinity of Marazion Green where she would materialise to the consternation of late travellers, for sometimes she would accompany them for a while before fading away and disappearing as mysteriously as she had originally appeared. I have not been able to trace the possible identity of the apparition.

Morwenstow

Psychic disturbances at nearby Tonacombe Manor have been described by Michael Williams who visited the fine fifteenth-century house with David Waddon-Martyn. Reported phenomena have included knockings on several windows and doors, apparently from within the house; the sound of material being

Mr and Mrs Ley, with the haunted Spanish chest

dragged across the floor; the misty image of an old lady in Stuart period costume; the form of a short, bald man, dressed in a black coat and breeches; and an Elizabethan woman carrying a big bunch of keys.

There are some grounds for thinking the ghostly old lady may be Katherine Kempthorne who may have died at Tonacombe in 1613 and lies buried in Morwenstow Church.

Some years ago strange happenings at Stanbury Manor were reported to me by the then occupant, Mr T A Ley, which seemed to centre on a large cedar chest which was thought to be of Spanish origin and possibly came to this country with the Spanish Armada. Carved on the lid and four sides were representations of dismembered heads and headless bodies. The proprietor of the shop where it was purchased had said there was 'something queer' about the chest: wherever it had been placed in the shop, things fell off the walls in the immediate vicinity. Mr Ley, until he could decide on a permanent place for the chest, had it put in the armoury.

The next morning, while he was walking through this room, six guns fell off the wall together – the wires were not broken and the hooks were still intact and secure.

The chest was moved into the Leys' bedroom. That same evening, while Mr Ley was helping his wife to hang some curtains on a four-poster bedstead, a picture fell down and struck him, although he was fully eighteen inches from the wall at the time. Oddly, the heavy picture hit Mr Ley on the head so lightly he hardly felt it, and it left no mark.

Next day three more pictures fell off the walls of the room containing the chest while Mr and Mrs Ley were actually present. Two days later four more pictures came down in the drawing-room, where the chest had been moved, again while both the occupants of the thirteenth-century house were present. One of these pictures went backwards through some stout pine panelling into a 'secret' passage.

Next day another picture fell in the drawing-room. In every case no hook or wire was broken, although many of the pictures which fell for no apparent reason were damaged.

The local press dubbed it 'the case of the poltergeist chest' and a former curate of Newlyn West, recognising the published photograph, related the following story about it.

Many years ago there lived in the village two ladies who owned the chest. They were both elderly and very deaf, and used to communicate by means of messages written on notepaper and passed to each other. They lived as recluses and were rarely seen in the village by the local people. During their lives they had collected a great deal of junk and thought they possessed a valuable collection of antiques. They decided to put these objects up for sale and the curate went along to examine the articles. He found it very difficult to do business with the deaf ladies, since they wrote their usual notes and expected him to reply in the same way.

On making enquiries among the inhabitants the curate learned that, when young, the two sisters had gone on a visit

43

to some friends and, arriving very late, they retired without unpacking their trunks which they placed on a chest that stood in the bedroom allocated to them. In the morning as they awakened, their attention was immediately drawn to the chest for, although weighed down by the heavy trunks, the lid was opening! They went over to the trunk and looked inside and what they saw was so horrible it is said they were struck deaf on the spot. What they had in fact seen they would never reveal.

On hearing this story I immediately remembered the account of a haunted chest published in a volume of 'authentic narratives' in London in 1882, entitled *Ghostly Visitors*. This story concerned a hard-headed surgeon who went to visit a friend at his house in the Midlands. The bedroom allocated to him was spacious but dreary, and in one corner stood a large carved chest. After examining the outside of the chest the surgeon, moved by some unexplained impulse, raised the lid. Inside he saw a man lying with his throat cut. With an exclamation of horror and surprise the surgeon let the lid fall, but almost immediately raised it again. To his great astonishment the chest was empty! On mentioning his experience to his host the next morning, the latter stared at him in amazement and informed the surgeon that a former occupant of the room had committed suicide and had been found in the chest in the condition now described by the visitor.

If it was the same chest, was a sight such as the surgeon witnessed horrible enough to strike two young women deaf? We know that a woman's hair turned white at Ilford in 1943 following an accident, and Marie Antoinette is said to have suffered in the same way. One wonders whether on re-opening the chest the ladies, too, found it empty – a fact which might well account for their never revealing what they had seen.

As far as the Leys' chest is concerned, Mr Ley told me there were no further disturbances. He wondered whether it had anything to do with the death of a member of the Ley family which seemed to coincide with the total cessation of anything unusual happening in the vicinity of the carved Spanish chest.

Mount's Bay

Here, according to the reports of many fishermen, a ghost voice calls the words 'I will ... I will' over and over again amid the occasional sound of church bells far out in the bay.

More than a hundred years ago there lived at nearby Ludgvan an old man named Polgrain and his young wife Sarah who, tiring of her elderly husband, became the lover of a young sailor known as Yorkshire Jack.

Sarah murdered her husband with arsenic and nearly got away with it. The local doctor was satisfied that death had been due to natural causes and signed the death certificate accordingly. After the funeral, however, as Sarah and her young lover lived together openly, rumours of foul play began to circulate and eventually the body of old Polgrain was exhumed and was found to be full of arsenic.

Sarah was arrested, charged with murder, found guilty and sentenced to be hanged. On the day of the public execution Sarah, as a last request, asked that Yorkshire Jack might be allowed to accompany her to the scaffold. Together they mounted the gallows platform and just as the rope was being placed around Sarah's neck, the couple embraced and kissed for the last time. Spectators near the gallows heard Sarah say, in slow and measured tones: 'You will – you promise you will?' to which Jack answered, nervously but firmly, 'I will – Sarah – I will...'

Soon after the execution of Sarah Polgrain her ghost was seen in Ludgvan: once in the churchyard where she and Jack had been in the habit of meeting and once or twice on the high road between Penzance and Hayle, where she and Jack had walked so many times and planned so many happy days ahead of them. But it was Jack who, apparently, saw the ghost of Sarah most often.

The once happy and carefree young sailor changed almost overnight and before long he was morose, short-tempered, restless and unhappy, and he developed a habit of constantly looking over his shoulder. To one or two old friends he confided,

'She gives me no peace…she is there, wherever I go…' And they knew he spoke of Sarah.

Even at sea Jack was haunted by his dead lover. His shipmates chaffed him for always turning and rebuking something they could not see, but at night as he lay in his hammock, silent, brooding, his eyes darting here and there, they said nothing for some of them also felt a strange and unpleasant presence to be there in their midst.

After weeks at sea Jack's ship returned home and, when they were once more in Mount's Bay, Jack, unhappy and restless as usual, evidently felt he must talk. He confided to his mates that Sarah, on the scaffold, had made him promise on his oath that on that very day, at midnight, he would marry her. Thinking to comfort her in her last moments, he had agreed; but ever since that day she had never left him and, he added in a hollow voice, 'not being able to wed me in the flesh, she means to bind me to her forever in death.'

That night, at midnight, the ship's company in the immediate vicinity were awakened by the sound of footsteps, light and tripping, like someone in high-heeled shoes. They traversed the passage leading to where Jack lay, unsleeping, in his hammock. Without a word, his features contorted with terror, he rose and climbed on deck, the tap-tap-tap of the footsteps following close behind him.

On deck Jack did not hesitate: he made straight for the bulwark, clambered up and leapt deliberately and helplessly into the sea...he was never seen again. As he disappeared some of his shipmates asserted they heard the far-off chiming of church bells and many of them believed they were hearing Jack's wedding bells; Sarah had kept Jack to his word. Ever since, over the years, there have been reports of phantom wedding bells being heard, far out in Mount's Bay, and what sounds like a forlorn voice calling 'I will... I will' before it is lost in the wind.

Mousehole

Amanda Casson told Marc Alexander, who has travelled extensively throughout Britain in his search for ghosts, that she (in common with other visitors) had a curious and totally inexplicable experience at The Ship Inn when she was staying there.

She had just had a bath and, on emerging from the bathroom, was walking down a long corridor when she saw the figure of a man leaning against the angle of the wall. He seemed to be

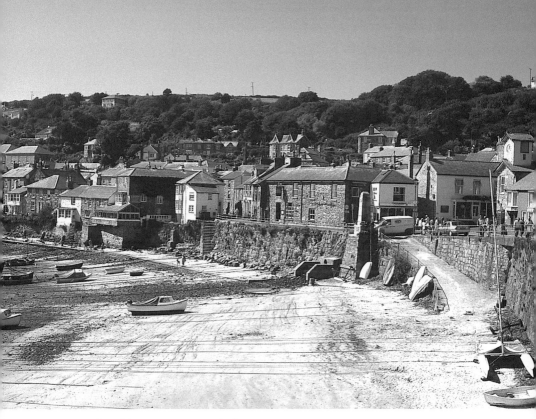

The Ship Inn at Mousehole

wearing present-day clothes of grey cloth, but as she approached him he simply faded away and the corridor was deserted. There was no question of his moving: she actually watched as he grew less and less distinct until there was nothing where seconds earlier there had been what appeared to be the solid and natural figure of a man.

Miss Casson, at that time manager of an employment bureau in London, asked the proprietors of The Ship whether anyone else had ever seen such a figure or had reported anything odd. No one seemed to know anything and there was, Miss Casson was told, no tradition of ghostly appearances at the inn.

Oddly enough my wife and I were having a drink at The Ship some years ago when we were staying at Marazion and we were chatting with another couple who were sharing our table, when the talk chanced to turn to ghosts. A local man who was standing nearby seemed to be interested in our conversation and after a few moments he came over and said he had once seen a ghost at The Ship.

It seemed he had been helping the owner with some structural repairs in the upper part of the old inn one Sunday afternoon when the place was empty. As he walked along the upper corridor he had looked up to see a man walking ahead of him. The man appeared to be perfectly normal and there was certainly nothing frightening about the form until, as the local man was wondering to himself who on earth it could be, the figure was suddenly no longer there.

He thought he must have imagined the whole thing but it was so real and so natural and ordinary that he was very puzzled. He had mentioned the incident to the owner who had poured such scorn on his story that he had hardly talked about the matter to anyone.

So it would seem there may be an unidentified ghost at The Ship who occasionally manifests for some unknown reason.

Newquay

Nearby Trerice, a property belonging to the National Trust but formerly owned for over four centuries by the Arundells, one of the great families of Cornwall, is a delightful house with a psychic fragrance and a gentle Grey Lady ghost.

A fascinating guide book to Newquay and the surrounding area, dating from the First World War, refers to Trerice as 'an ancient baronial mansion which the country people still declare to be haunted by the unhouseled spirit of a certain passionate Lord of Arundell, known in the neighbouring villages as "the wicked lord"... a delightful survival of the picturesque old days and the very ideal of an old haunted mansion ... grey, venerable, hedged in with dark cypresses dotting the moss-grown lawn... The north wing of the old house was pulled down in the latter part of the nineteenth century, as no one would live in it, and all the personal possessions of the "wicked lord", his desk, papers, hunting and other gear, hurriedly burnt. For more than a century the place was left untouched...' And it is in the restored north wing that several psychic disturbances have been reported in recent years.

When I was last there in 1981 the north wing had only been open a few years and during alterations a number of unexplained happenings were reported. Doors opened by themselves; a 'presence' was distinctly felt by prosaic workmen; 'something' made a swishing sound along the old floorboards, reminiscent of someone passing by in a crinoline. Then there is the mysterious 'whiff of perfume' and the occasional appearance of a Grey Lady who walks the north wing, along the Gallery, and disappears down the stone circular stairway that once led to the original entrance to the house. Could all these happenings have any connection, one wonders, with the vague stories of the 'wicked lord' seducing a young servant girl and of her subsequent suicide?

Several of the guides over the years have told me they have noticed an 'inexplicable fragrance' (resembling lilac) on occasions and sometimes they have had the distinct impression someone or something had passed close by when no visible form was there. A former administrator of Trerice tells me there is a story of violent death at the house, fairly well substantiated, concerning a stable lad who was killed when some horses stampeded across the courtyard. His ghost had repeatedly, I am told, been seen in the area of the courtyard.

Many visitors to Trerice comment upon the atmosphere of the house: some have sensed the presence of death in the Library; some have felt they 'stepped back in time' when they walked through the Gallery; one or two visitors have been so affected by the invisible influences in the Hall that they have left the house – but for the vast majority of the thousands of visitors who come to see beautiful Trerice every year, it is a place of peace and happiness, a welcome refuge for a while from life's hustle and bustle.

Padstow

Built about 1580 and lived in continuously ever since, The White Hart in Padstow is reputedly the oldest inn – although it is no longer a hostelry. Julie Frost, who moved into the premises with her husband Fred and two young sons in the 1950s, didn't give a second thought to vague stories of ghosts and ghostly happenings. The family soon acquired a dog, Crispin, and two cats, Bobo and Mister Moses. Julie later described Crispin as 'a mixture of spaniel and retriever – a real tough guy', Bobo as 'every inch a lady, fastidious and gentle', and Moses as 'the bad lad of the trio – a spiv, and none too bright…'

Nevertheless it was through the behaviour of their pets that the Frost family first became aware of peculiar happenings at The White Hart. Why, the whole family found themselves wondering, did Bobo sit in the window at dusk, eagerly looking out and seeing 'something' they couldn't see and welcoming 'it' with little chirruping sounds and purrs? She must be looking at the bats swooping about, they decided, but if this was so why did she run to the door and go walking round, tail erect, as if rubbing against the legs of a friend? And how was it that one day during a violent storm, when all the doors and windows were firmly closed and latched, she arrived indoors, wet, before she could be admitted? And when a neighbourhood rogue cat pinned her down on a nearby roof, who pitched a stone so skilfully that her tormentor was sent flying? Certainly no human being was in the area at the time.

Then there were footsteps. The heavy oak front door led into a passage and the vast iron bolt was always secured at dusk. Time after time all the family would hear footfalls pass the living room door and proceed upstairs. Once Julie was actually on the stairs when the footsteps began to approach with measured tread… She felt nothing. No sensation of coldness, no icy draught, no feeling of a 'presence', yet whatever it was must have passed at very close quarters, for the footsteps continued on up the stairs beyond her. In the bitter winter of 1963 Fred was the first member of the family to hear the strange breathing sound that soon became known as the 'iron lung' – an artificial respirator. It was a hollow, unpleasant, penetrating sound. Fred was in an upstairs room that first time and the sound seemed to emanate from a nearby bedroom; he walked quickly into the room – to be met by complete and utter silence.

The Frost family kept to themselves the strange happenings they were experiencing and they never spoke of them to anyone outside the immediate family. But one day, out of the blue, a neighbour began to tell them about some historical research he had been carrying out concerning his own house. In fact, he had learned little about his own property, but he had discovered that many years earlier a priest, unable to find a bed at the nearby clerics' resthouse in St Edmund's Lane, had taken a bed at The White Hart. He had been an asthmatic and had fallen victim to a fearful attack during the night, and had died. The rasping noise the occupants of The White Hart had so recently heard sounded just like someone having an asthmatic attack, they felt, and it was surely much more likely to be that than an iron lung.

The haunted family began to call their unbidden guest 'Wilfred' for no good reason, but simply to put a name to it. Wilfred seemed to like milk bottles: on numerous occasions when the bottles were put out in the passage at night, 'he' would move them to the other side of the passage; not every night, but it happened two or three times a month without fail.

And then there were the door movements. One fine summer evening when there was not a breath of wind, the heavy oak door that had been closed but not bolted opened by itself and gently swayed to and fro, creaking quietly. On and on it went until Fred Frost gently closed it and held it in position – and it shook and vibrated like a living thing beneath his hand. When Julie exchanged her hand for that of her husband's, it instantly became less active, ceased all movement and became what it was, still, dead wood.

Over the years there have been occupants of The White Hart who have neither heard nor felt anything unusual there; people perhaps who are not on the 'wavelength' that enables them to be in rapport with the supernormal. When two old ladies, the Misses Reynolds, lived there, however, they were very much aware of odd happenings and especially of inexplicable footsteps. Times without number they would hear distinct footfalls in the front passage and sometimes they would look out but they never saw anything, or if they did they never said so. They also heard footsteps – for which there was no possible explanation – mount the stairs and gradually fade away. They never heard the footsteps come down the stairs and, although it was rather disturbing, they never felt there was really anything to be frightened of. They used to say they liked the house but not the noises the house made!

In 1964 the property was up for sale and another two women, this time a mother and daughter, came to view the place. Both were strangers to the district and neither knew anything about the house; yet as they were leaving the older woman said, with the conviction of years and in a tone that brooked no opposition: 'This place is haunted.' Another prospective buyer had left her shopping in one of the rooms while she looked round the rest of the empty house; when she returned she found that all her groceries had been removed from her bag and their individual wrappings, and everything was arranged in a neat circle on the floor. She did not buy the property!

At that time the electrical system in the house left much to be desired; there were no such things as two-way switches and the last person to bed made their way upstairs in darkness, having switched off the downstairs light. One night Fred, who was usually the last to retire, arrived upstairs oddly shaken. He had switched off the light on the landing and had set off up the last short flight of stairs, as he had done scores of times before. At least he intended to do that, but the moment the light was out he felt he was lost although he was on thoroughly familiar ground. He described the sensation as feeling as though he was 'in a vacuum, a strange and timeless limbo'. There was complete loss of mental and physical orientation and a depth of darkness

53

such as he had never known before that night. Although it sounds trivial, in fact the experience was distinctly distasteful and distressing. Eventually he eased his way along the wall to the switch, having no idea how long he had been 'lost' or why he had not called out; but next day he bought the most powerful torch in Padstow and never went to bed again without it!

Some months later the Frost family heard with interest the experience of a man who had once lived alone at The White Hart; an experience of a very similar nature but he apparently blundered into a furnished room and he described in some detail the contents and lay-out: in fact there was no such room or furniture in the house.

After the Frosts left The White Hart the house was temporarily empty and during this period some workmen carrying out repairs reported they had distinctly seen the figures of two people in an upstairs room. Knowing the house was empty and locked, they had taken steps to make sure no one had broken in. Needless to say, no one had.

In relating her experiences of life at The White Hart thirty years earlier, Mrs Frost told me in 1982 that she had not mentioned the few, but memorable, unpleasant happenings she had never forgotten, adding: 'I loved that house, but now I am a widow living alone, I don't think I would care to return...'

In September 1982 I explored the ancient Abbey House on North Quay; for the first time in its long history this quaint and sombre and mysterious house was open to the public. Abbey House has long been reputed to harbour a gentle ghost.

Prior to my visit I had talked with a long-standing resident of Padstow who told me she remembered hearing stories of the place being haunted when she was a girl. As a child she and her friends always passed Abbey House quietly, forever looking over their shoulders, and almost on tiptoe, in order not to disturb the ghost!

Abbey House is undoubtedly one of the oldest houses in Cornwall and records tell of it being an old house when Sir Walter Raleigh held his court on the South Quay during the reign of Queen Elizabeth I. Abbey House was the Guild House in the fifteenth century and the merchants of Padstow, who financed ventures from their busy port to Brittany and elsewhere, met there. Its name suggests an ecclesiastical connection but no one seems to know why the house is so named although, of course, Padstow was at one time a centre of Celtic Christianity. A thousand years ago the monastic community moved to Bodmin, following repeated raids by the warring Danes, but the monks retained an interest in Padstow, still owning much of the town, with the rest in the ownership of the Bishop. After Henry VIII dissolved the monasteries, Abbey House and much of Padstow was purchased by Nicholas Prideaux, Steward of the Prior of Bodmin, and the house remained the property of the Prideaux family until 1938.

As I wandered through this building so full of memories, I learned that the ghost is thought to be that of a girl or young woman; an Elizabethan who climbs the fifteenth-century granite newel staircase from the age-old cellar, with its blocked-up tunnel running to Prideaux Place, and makes her silent way along the time-worn passage in the oldest part of this old house. Some people have detected a sense of loneliness and sadness in these parts of Abbey House, as though the girl is saying, 'Nobody loves me ... nobody cares about me...' The model of an Elizabethan girl, a red wax figure dating from about 1620 and exhibited at that time in the house, I found strangely evocative and could even represent, I felt, the ghost of Abbey House.

Par

A ghost with a difference may haunt Daphne du Maurier's old home, the Rashleigh mansion, 'Menabilly'. She told my friend Joseph Braddock that a ghostly 'lady in blue' had been haunting the house since Edwardian times; a gentle, quiet, harmless figure that was only ever seen looking out of a certain bedroom window.

The famous author of *Rebecca*, *Jamaica Inn*, *Vanishing Cornwall* and so many other wonderful books made extensive enquiries over a long period, but she was never able to definitely establish who this 'lady in blue' might be and then a novel thought struck her. Could the ghost be not a phantom from the past but a peep into the future? When Daphne du Maurier came to write *The King's General*, she wrote it in the room where the ghostly lady was reputed to appear. As she worked, the authoress would herself rest from time to time and look out of that very window for inspiration, and she invariably wore her blue working smock! It amused her to think that those who had said they had seen the 'lady in blue' as they walked across the sweeping lawns in 1910 and over the succeeding years might have seen, not a ghost from the past, but herself in 1945!

In her latter years Daphne du Maurier left her beloved Menabilly and lived at the Dower House, Kilmarth, half a mile away. Her longtime housekeeper and companion, Esther Rowe, told me in 1993 that she had often been conscious of the presence of the complex and place-obsessed Daphne du Maurier in the vicinity of her last home.

Penryn

Just before Christmas a phantom coach and horses is said to drive through this town: some people say the horses are headless, some say the driver has no head, and some say the story dates back to the days of smuggling… but why only once a year, a few days before Christmas?

Another ghost was immortalised here in a melodrama entitled *The Penryn Tragedy*. The story goes that after long years at sea a sailor returned to his native town to see his old parents who ran an inn. For a joke the returning son thought he would fool the old people for a while. So he disguised himself and booked a room at the inn, where he was taken for a rich man who had come to Penryn by accident and was known to no one and no one knew he was there. In fact he had confided his idea of a joke to his sister who lived in another part of Penryn.

The innkeeper and his wife decided to murder their unknown guest while he was the worse for drink, to gain possession of the money they believed he carried with him. Only after they had committed the crime did they recognise the dead man as their son.

The shock and horror at what they had done caused them both to commit suicide and their daughter died of a broken heart soon afterwards. For years the place was reported to be unquiet at dead of night: heavy thumps and bangs sounded in the stillness, strange whisperings were borne away on the night air and terrifying sighs and groans disturbed the quiet of night and echoed in the darkness.

Penzance

'Oh yes, we've got a ghost here all right,' my wife and I were told when we called at The Dolphin Inn, one of Cornwall's oldest inns; 'in fact two ghosts...'

The best-known ghost visitor is thought to be an old sea captain who died here, and those who claim to have seen the ghost form describe it as a swarthy figure wearing a tricorn hat, lace ruffles and with brass buttons on his coat. A previous landlord's wife saw 'the Captain', or 'George' as he is variously called, several times and it is not unknown for a visitor, without knowing anything about the reputed ghost, to ask about the formidable old sea-dog they thought they caught a glimpse of. More frequently they will ask about the ghostly footsteps which have been heard many times by reputable witnesses.

Over the years both landlords and their wives have heard the heavy, measured tread, marching across the ceiling and sometimes continuing down the stairs. It always seems to begin in the front and original upper part of the inn, pass over the bar and disappear towards the back of the building. At the rear of the inn's main cellar, there is an open space, rather like the bottom of a lift shaft and here in 1873 a young man was killed in an unfortunate accident. His phantom form is reputed to be the second ghost at The Dolphin.

Within recent memory the figure of a young man with fair hair has also been seen in one of the bedrooms. Mary Clark saw

him twice in one week, but it is not known whether he or 'the Captain' is responsible for another psychic manifestation here.

In room 4 a mysterious depression is often noticed in a cushion that rests on a certain chair, exactly as though someone has just been sitting there. No matter how often the cushion is shaken up and replaced, even when the room is unused and locked, the indentation always reappears. Next door, in room 5, a somewhat similar indentation has been seen in the bed and pillow, almost as though someone invisible is sleeping or resting there.

From time to time other odd things have been noticed at the inn: traces of the old-fashioned coarse tobacco; a dragging noise; and the sound of whispering from empty rooms. Sir John Hawkins set up his headquarters here in 1588 when he was enlisting Cornishmen to fight the Spanish Armada and there must have been many whispered conversations in those turbulent days. Some years ago a secret hiding place was discovered, still containing two casks of rum, and there is little doubt The Dolphin was once a smugglers' inn. There must have been many times when a dragging noise was heard here at dead of night in those days. On the other hand, Judge Jeffreys held court here in what is now the dining room, while the prisoners were kept in the cellars, so it may be from those far off days that the dragging noise originated. As for the old-fashioned tobacco, well, it is said Sir Walter Raleigh enjoyed the first pipe of tobacco to be smoked in England at The Dolphin!

Chapel Street is reputed to be haunted by the ghost of old Mrs Baines who was mistaken for a thief and was shot. Her figure is said to be seen on occasions, wearing a dark cloak and bonnet, at the top of the street and disappearing into a wall.

An old house in Morrab Road, once a doctors' surgery and later an old people's home, has long been said to be haunted. During the latter period a number of curious happenings were reported, including the shadowy form of a man standing beside a bedroom window. This unidentified ghost was seen by several members of the staff of the home and also by patients and visitors. He is thought to be the ghost of a dead doctor who was so dedicated to his patients that even death cannot give him rest; possibly he is the first resident doctor at the home – certainly the sightings date from his death.

Fairly recently two girl babysitters, knowing nothing of the history of the house or the reputed ghost, saw a man walk along the hall and disappear into the room that once served as a surgery. They investigated immediately but found the room completely deserted. Later that night they again both saw the same figure traverse the same area and afterwards they refused to babysit in the house – a very understandable decision.

Perranporth

A wooden cabin on a caravan site here was reported by several occupants and by the camp owner to be haunted.

Peter Moss recounts the experience of two ladies who were disturbed at night by the sound of stealthy footsteps padding round the outside of the building, although they saw nothing. Suddenly the front door, which they had been careful to close and lock, burst open and then slammed shut, all of its own accord; and then the padding sounds seemed to emanate from inside the cabin, in fact from the living room next door to the bedroom occupied by the two frightened women! One of them called out 'Who the devil are you?' and this produced a sudden and complete silence.

Moments later they heard the sound of rustling papers and a quiet chuckle, as though someone was enjoying what they were reading.

The rustle and crinkle of paper were heard again, followed by another chuckle and then a noise that sounded like something breaking. Plucking up their courage the two puzzled visitors looked at each other and then got out of their beds and threw open the door – the living room was completely deserted but a rocking chair was swaying to and fro as though someone was seated in it.

The steady rhythm continued and again they both heard a chuckle and the rustle of invisible paper. As they went into the room they seemed to sense the low growl of an unseen animal, situated somewhere behind the still moving rocking chair. The two ladies had had enough. They fled back to their bedroom and remained huddled together until dawn.

At first light they packed their cases and set out to see the camp owner who told them she was not surprised, for she had heard similar reports from other visitors. She offered the two women the use of a luxury caravan for the rest of their stay and there they passed their time peacefully and uneventfully.

Perranzabuloe

A ghost story that smacks of a dream caused by a guilty conscience is told of an old woman who found a set of false teeth protruding from the soil in Perranzabuloe churchyard. Thinking she might find a use for them, she picked them up, took them home and placed them in her bedroom.

That night, she always said, she was awakened from her sleep by noises outside her cottage window and a spectral voice

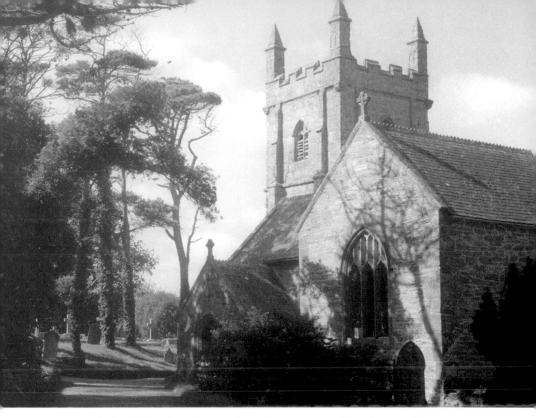

Perranzabuloe Church, where a ghost is very possessive of its teeth

demanding over and over again: 'Give me back my teeth! Give me back my teeth!' Hastily snatching up the wretched teeth, the old woman flung them out of the window, without daring to look at whatever might be there, but when the teeth left her hand, the noises and the voice ceased and she heard footsteps going away from the house in the direction of the churchyard.

Next morning, before anyone was about, she searched the soft ground outside her window and the muddy roadway but of the teeth there was no sign; nor were there any footprints or any marks that might account for the sounds she had heard during the night.

As folklorist Christina Hole said to me as she told me this story: 'The old woman never heard the voice or the footsteps again, nor, I imagine, did she ever again bring back any finds from the churchyard!'

Polperro

A correspondent tells me he heard two men talking about a smuggler's ghost which haunted the caves here. There is a story that two fair-traders fell out over the sharing of some gold and, in the fight that followed, one of them was killed. Thereafter his ghost haunted the cave, looking for his fair share of the gold that belonged to neither of them.

Certainly there are persistent reports of a dark form being seen in the caves by local people and visitors alike. One of the phantoms that is reputed to wander among the maze of tunnels behind the cavern below Chapel Hill on the west side of the harbour is thought to be that of Willy Willcock. He was a fisherman who set out to explore the subterranean labyrinth and was never seen again. His ghost is reported to be seen and heard on dark and quiet nights, his ghostly cries, the shrieks of a dying man, issuing from the mouth of the cave where he starved to death, within a stone's throw of the cave entrance.

Porthtowan

On that part of the road to Portreath known as Chapel Hill stands Woodlands Restaurant, which was formerly known as the Dog and Dragon.

The story behind this strange name is that many, many years ago the neighbourhood was greatly troubled by a fire-breathing dragon which regularly stole and ate sheep and cattle. One May Eve, formerly a great festival for the return of life and virility, just before midnight, the dragon was met by a huge white, spotted dog that growled a warning. As the dragon went for the nearest sheep, the dog sank its teeth into the hind-quarters of the dragon and the fight was on. The dragon tried to catch the dog as it snapped again and again at the dragon's tail. Round and round they flew, the dragon becoming more and more angry and confused until the sun began to rise and the dog, with sudden determination, tore off the tip of the dragon's tail. The monster gave a terrible howl of pain and disappeared in the

Does the ancient legend of the dog and the dragon have anything to do with the mysterious spectral dog which has been seen near Porthtowan?

direction of the sea and was never seen again.

An ancient 'dragon-path' or 'ley' runs through the lands where the restaurant now stands – but all this can surely have no connection with the mysterious spectral dog that has been seen hereabouts from time to time?

Oddly enough most of the sightings correspond with the festival nights of the old Celtic calendar: Midsummer, Midwinter, Beltane, Hallow-e'en, Candlemas Day and Lammas-tide, but most frequently, it seems, on May Eve.

Portreath

When I was here a year or two ago, I was told about a phantom man who occasionally appeared in the vicinity of a corner seat of a restaurant. It stood on the site of a large old stone building which in past years had been used for storing fishing and boating tackle.

In earlier days, however, it had been used, not infrequently, as a temporary morgue for the many unidentified and unclaimed bodies that were always being washed ashore during gales. Any unclaimed bodies were laid to rest with a headstone bearing the date and such words as 'unknown sailor'. It is thought the still figure seen at Portreath has the air of waiting for someone, perhaps for some loved one, to come and claim his body for burial.

Smugglers Cottage near the beach has long been considered to be haunted. Many years ago a small secret closet was uncovered during the course of alterations. The closet contained a small table, the skeleton of a man and the remains of his black cloak, an ancient sea chest and an old sword. The sword and the table were presented to the Exeter Museum.

Whether the skeleton has any connection with the ghost of the slight young man, dressed in what has been described as 'Jacobean style', is not known, but the discovery of the human remains made no difference to the appearances of the ghost which is usually described as appearing out of the wall panelling in a corridor on the first floor and walking 'furtively' towards the stairs, where 'he' vanishes. The place where the ghost appears is said to be the original entrance to a tunnel leading down to the beach.

The ghost was reportedly seen by two nurses and a dog on one occasion, and ten years later by a visitor who thought a fancy-dress dance must be taking place somewhere in the vicinity.

A few years earlier a party of ghost-hunters spent four hours of darkness and discomfort in the haunted passage and were rewarded by a sudden drop in the temperature at 1.30 a.m. and at the same time a dog, accompanying the watchers, seemed to sense something invisible to its human companions

Poundstock

Beautiful Penfound Manor has been the scene of apparently ghostly manifestations, which have usually been associated with Kate Penfound who lived here during the Civil War.

Kate was in love with John Trebarfoot of nearby Trebarfoot Manor, but he and his family supported Cromwell while the Penfounds were Royalists. When neither Kate nor John could convince their respective families that love was more important than politics, the young couple decided to elope. One April evening, traditionally the 26th, Kate made her way through the window of her bedroom into the arms of her waiting lover. But Arthur Penfound, Kate's father, suddenly faced the couple in the courtyard and in the fight that followed both Kate and John died.

Some say that Penfound in his blind anger shot both his daughter and her lover; others say that in attempting to come between John and her father, Kate was shot and the men fought on and killed each other.

At all events each April 26th the ghost of Kate Penfound is said to appear and rejoin her lover John in the courtyard, and at other times her father has been seen in various parts of this utterly charming and atmospheric house. Sometimes Kate's white face has reportedly been seen, peering from the window in her bedroom, looking for her lover, as she must have looked

65

A tragic story of star-crossed lovers lies behind the reputed haunting of Penfound Manor, near Poundstock

three hundred years ago, little thinking they would both be dead by the arm of her father within an hour or so.

Previous occupants of Penfound Manor asserted they sometimes heard distinct voices; and the son of a former tenant maintains he saw the ghostly form of Kate on several occasions, crossing the Great Hall on her way towards the main stairs. To my knowledge there have been no sightings of the ghosts and no manifestations of any kind in recent years. However, some former residents told me they were occasionally disturbed by the sound of voices and odd bangs and crashing sounds coming from the direction of Kate's bedroom and the courtyard below, which must be much as it was when two people who passionately loved one another died there.

The church of St Neot at Poundstock is reputed to be haunted by the ghost of a murdered priest. William Penfound was celebrating Mass in December 1356, when several parishioners entered the church and, for some unknown reason, murdered the priest. The two ringleaders, named as John Bevill and Simon de St Gennys, were arrested and stood trial, but were pardoned – one cannot help pondering on the story that must lie behind the deed and the pardon. No wonder that to this day the ghostly form of the Reverend William Penfound is said to be seen sometimes, wandering among the graves and inside the church he loved.

Praa Sands

Several very ancient legends are associated with Pengersick involving magic swords, witches, a magic white hare and the elixir of life. In later days, John Milliton, who rebuilt the place as a fortified manor, is thought by some people to haunt the house where he tried to murder his wife with poisoned wine, but she craftily changed goblets. Another story is that, while they were dining together, Milliton suddenly announced he had poisoned his wife's drink: whereupon she replied in that case they would both die, for she had poisoned his! Of such activities ghosts are born.

Pengersick Castle was once occupied by the violent Henry de Pengersick, known as Henry le Fort, who was excommunicated for attacking and wounding a vicar and a monk, among his other virtues.

The present owner, Mrs Angela Evans, and her son Guy, live

at the restored and historic but haunted castle, although they have not themselves had any paranormal experiences; however other people have. A neighbour has seen a ghost monk walk through the bordering wall, and an annual visitor has seen what she believes to be the ghost of the fourteenth-century Engrina Pengersick in one of the bedrooms. The present occupants have told me, 'If ghosts there are here, we would be inclined to think they could well be Henry Pengersick, later Henry le Fort, and Engrina Pengersick.' In 1997 an investigation was carried out by The Ghost Club Society and, during the course of the full all-night study, seven of the ten saw two ghostly female figures. The remaining three all felt 'something' was in the room; in actual fact these three were so positioned that they did not have the same view as the rest of the investigating team.

The full story of haunted Pengersick Castle and the investigation, with evidence of two phantom figures, video film of strange lights and odd markings on a slate are detailed in the booklet *Pengersick Castle* by Trevor Kenward and Robert Snow.

Roche Rock

A ruined fifteenth-century chapel, set high among this rocky outcrop, is reputed to be haunted by the ghost of a man who sometimes stares angrily from his lofty perch. Certainly many visitors to this strange spot have reported seeing a shadowy figure moving among the rocks. At first they have thought a real person is up there casting a shadow and then they have realised the 'shadow' can be seen in different positions and from different directions, and that it resembles a man, bent over and hurrying about the rocks.

Some people say the ghost is that of a miner, others that he was a leper, and others again – since this is Cornwall – that he was a smuggler. A few visitors to this isolated place have remarked upon strange sounds they have heard apparently emanating from the chapel ruin.

A correspondent from Warminster has told me of her experience with a boyfriend in the days when visitors were allowed to

*Pengersick Castle, beside Mount's Bay, was the scene of historic violence.
In 1997, during an all-night investigation, seven out of the ten
investigators saw two ghostly figures*

risk life and limb on the rocks. The couple had discovered the place some years previously and Mark, her boyfriend, loved it because it was so climbable and risky. My informant, Nicola, tells me she was less keen, as it always felt rather cold and decidedly unsafe. On this occasion they both climbed the first ladder and after looking around Mark decided he was going higher. Nicola felt cold and called to Mark to say she was going back to the car. He replied he would be down in a few moments.

After waiting some ten minutes in the car, Nicola thought she'd take a photograph of Mark on the Rock. She saw a figure in the windows, so she took a couple of snaps and then waved. There was no response to her wave and then she saw Mark on the top of the Rock, waving. She took another photograph and then looked back to the window where the silhouette figure was still visible. She soon realised it could not be a person because there was no flooring or ceiling behind the window. She decided to join Mark, hoping he would tell here there was someone else up there, but she felt a sudden and severe coldness and she just

could not climb the Rock. She called to Mark and hurried back to the car. When Mark joined her he said there had not been anyone else on the Rock.

When the film was taken to be developed, Nicola discovered that each of the three shots of Roche were blank. The camera was a basic one without lens cap and so on. All the preceding shots were fine and the subsequent shots were all present and correct. Nicola tells me all this may be trivial and circumstantial, but the strongly hostile feeling on that sunny afternoon was very real and left her anxious for several days afterwards. Nicola adds that neither she nor Mark knew anything about the history of Roche Rock until afterwards, but 'if it is one of those places which absorbed an atmosphere from the monks who lived there, they must have been a miserable lot!'

St Germans

The good St German, it is said, came to Cornwall in the reign of the free-thinking orthodox Catholic Roman Emperor Valentinian. But his doctrines of freewill and the value of good works, and his many remarkable miracles, met stiff opposition: he was persecuted by some of the priests and monks and by many of the local people.

One Sunday, while he was attending to his pious duties, a brawl developed and he was set upon. Eventually he escaped and fled to a lonely place where he prayed for his persecutors. So intense was the agony and soul-suffering of this holy man that it is recorded the very rocks felt the power of his sadness 'and wept with him'. The weeping rocks were known as the Well of St German.

The parish has associations with early Christianity in Britain and was the original seat of the Cornish bishopric. It was the see of Bishop Burhwold who died in 1027, and Bishop Leofric founded a priory here.

Has the ghost monk that has long haunted the area walked for more than nine centuries? Certainly there are many stories and accounts of a ghost monk being encountered at St Germans.

In October 1982 a former resident told me the ghost was well known in the vicinity and it had been encountered by many people; a lonely, pathetic, harmless figure that was often taken for a real monk but sometimes it was recognised as a ghost, especially, it seems, by children. My informant told me that a few years ago, during a party for children at Port Eliot (the medieval and embattled mansion next to the Abbey Church), the ghost monk put in an appearance and was seen by some of the adults and by many of the children. The party was abandoned.

St Ives

Elliott O'Donnell once told me of a new house he rented for a time here where he was repeatedly disturbed at night by the sound of clinking footsteps that halted outside his door. Then he would hear a loud knock on the top panel of the door, followed by complete silence. Time after time O'Donnell would throw open the door but he never saw anything. Invariably all sounds would cease as soon as he opened the door, but there could be no doubt about the distinctive tap of approaching footsteps, suggesting a person wearing high-heeled shoes, and the sharp knock on the upper part of the bedroom door. The other disturbances, reported by O'Donnell and by later occupants, were the sound of doors opening and closing at dead of night and of footsteps mounting the stairs, but they were never heard descending.

One night O'Donnell sprinkled the passage outside his bedroom door with flour and sand alternately, and he fixed a line of cotton, breast-high, across the passage. The footsteps came that night as before, but the cotton was unbroken and the flour and sand showed no sign of any disturbance. Several housekeepers employed by O'Donnell left because of the strange goings on. Elliott O'Donnell, a keen student himself of all aspects of psychic phenomena, believed the land on which the house had been built attracted elementals and that they subsequently manifested inside the house.

The famous bay of St Ives has long been said to be haunted by phantom bells. There is also reputed to be a ghost ship that appears in the bay from time to time firing distress rockets, but when the would-be rescuers manage to get almost alongside the old-fashioned ship, it suddenly vanishes. Another story is told of a ship in distress in the bay, a real ship this time, the *Neptune* out of London, but by the time the local men reached the spot, the vessel had sunk beneath the waves – in the very place where the phantom ship had vanished.

Among the many unfortunate ships wrecked off the coast here one carried a passenger who, as the ship went down, clasped her baby and leapt for the safety of the lifeboats. But the heavy seas swept the child from her arms and away into the darkness of the sea and storm.

The mother was pulled out of the sea, more dead than alive, but she never recovered from the tragic loss of her baby. At her funeral some of the mourning folk of St Ives said they saw the figure of a woman float away from the grave towards the open sea.

For many years there have been stories of the sad figure of a woman searching for her baby along the shore on dark and stormy nights; a figure that disappears seawards whenever it is approached.

There is a haunted beach at St Ives. One summer morning a Society for Psychical Research member, Mrs Pauline Clare, saw a boat land, full of bearded men. They obviously didn't see her and, although they huddled together, talking anxiously, she could not hear any sound of voices. The beach seemed shorter and steeper than she remembered it. Presently the men made their way uphill towards the cliff.

Several years later Mrs Clare related her experience to another Cornishwoman, Mrs Day, who told her she had once had a curious experience at St Ives as well. Sitting with other young people at the top of a cliff she had seen a group of bearded men wearing long robes clamber up the cliff. Once at the top they formed a circle, kneeling down to reverence one man who stood in the middle. A boy beside her asked, 'What are you looking at?' and she replied she was watching the men. When he said, 'What men?', they vanished.

Mrs Clare tells me she checked that the cliff was the same one she had seen, and realised that if the men she saw had scrambled all the way up the cliff they could have come out just where Mrs Day saw them. She wondered whether some Cornish race memory held the picture or perhaps the imprint was simply in the place itself.

St Just-in-Penwith

An inn in the Pendeen-Botallack area was and perhaps still is haunted on the anniversary of a fight to the death. My informant's grandfather lodged at the inn and after work he was in the habit of sitting and reading or having a chat with the landlord in the evenings.

One night the landlord suggested he might like to go for a walk but after a hard day's work the lodger felt tired and put his feet up instead. He sensed the landlord grow more and more uneasy and then suddenly, without any warning, there was a tremendous thumping noise from the room above and the sound of fighting. The beams moved and shuddered under the violent movements. All of a sudden the door of an upstairs room burst open followed by the sound of a man falling heavily down the stairs – then silence.

The lodger, alarmed and puzzled, rose to his feet to see what had happened, but the landlord restrained him, saying there was nothing he could do and there were to be no more disturbances. Apparently many years earlier two brothers had fought savagely in the room above and one had been killed. Each year on the anniversary of the event the sound of the struggle was heard and the floorboards were seen to strain and move as long as the fight persisted, but after the sound of the losing combatant falling down the stairs all was quiet until the following year.

Feeling he would lose lodgers if it was known the house was haunted, the landlord had always tried to persuade his lodgers to be out of the house on the night of the anniversary – and he usually succeeded. My informant told me her grandfather had lived to a great age; she remembered hearing of the ghostly fight when she was very young. He always told the same story of the events of that night which remained a vivid and lasting memory for the rest of his life.

St Levan

A ghostly bell that seems to emanate from a sea captain's grave is said to foretell the death of anyone unfortunate enough to hear it, and there is a ghostly woman in a white garment also haunting the churchyard.

The haunted grave is that of Captain Richard Wetherall who perished when his brig *Aurora* sank in December 1811. It is said a seafaring man will hear the muffled sound of eight bells, signifying that his life's 'watch' will soon be over.

The ghostly woman in white walks on summer evenings and dates back several centuries and is still seen occasionally, but who she is and why she walks I have been unable to discover.

The old manor house of Penrose, near Sennen

Doubtless some of the reported sightings of this ghost have a natural explanation, but at least one encounter related to me firsthand seems quite impossible to explain away in rational terms.

Sennen

Nearby Penrose was once a manor house and the home of a family of that name. Some three or four hundred years ago seafaring Ralph Penrose was broken-hearted when his wife died of a fever. He left Penrose more and more in the care of his brother John, and went to sea, taking with him his seven-year-old son and his cousin William.

One night their ship ran into a storm and foundered in sight of home. Flares warned John and other local people what was happening but, on John's instructions, they stood and watched and did nothing to help. Only the boy, true heir to Penrose, survived it seemed. He was washed up on the shore but then callously murdered by John Penrose who then took over the house and the lands as his own.

However, unknown to anyone, William too had survived but with no memory of anything before the shipwreck.

He wandered far and wide until one day, quite by chance, he turned up at Penrose and heard the boy's voice which said: 'My uncle murdered me…I lie beneath the dead tree in the orchard…avenge the murder of your cousin's son…dig, and give me peace…'

William sought out a trusted friend and together they unearthed the remains of the murdered boy. They carried them by night to Sennen churchyard and there buried what was left of the little body.

Back at Penrose they found the body of John, hanging from a beam. He had hanged himself in sight of the disturbed grave of the innocent boy he had murdered.

William settled for a time at Penrose but before long he found the place to be so haunted that he gave up his rights to it and went away forever.

Sennen Cove is haunted by a ghost known as 'the Irish lady'. The story goes that she was the sole survivor of an Irish ship which foundered here. She managed to swim to a rock and haul herself to safety – or so she thought, but the sea was so rough it was impossible to rescue her. For several days and nights people on shore watched helplessly as she waved imploringly at them to save her.

Eventually she died from thirst, hunger and exposure, and the waves washed her body back into the sea. Ever since, when the waves run high at Sennen Cove, the ghostly form of 'the Irish lady' is seen clinging desperately to the rock that now bears her name.

Sennen Cove has also long been reputed to be haunted by phantom bells. Stanley Baron is just one witness who has told me of the eerie sound that has been heard by many people over the years. Stanley was staying with a local family and one night, just after eleven o'clock, having composed an article for the national daily to which he regularly contributed, he went to bed. But not to sleep; he seemed to toss and turn all night, he said possibly because he was over-tired. The sea-sprayed sands of the bay were a stone's throw from his window and, about one o'clock, he began to realise that in addition to the usual sounds of the sea there was a rhythmic clanging of bells. All this continued until about three o'clock, when he fell into a deep sleep.

At four o'clock, as he saw from his bedside clock, he was awakened by the long, low pealing of distant and muffled bells. Gradually their chiming diminished with the coming of the dawn.

At breakfast Stanley asked his hosts whether they had been awakened during the night by the sound of bells. 'They must have been the Lost Land Bells you heard...' he was told. Of course, he thought, the Lost Land, the Drowned Land of Lyonesse, with its seven score churches; drowned according to Cornish tradition, in two mighty surges of ocean, one in 1014 and the other in 1094.

The palace and gardens of Versailles, France, were the scene of a remarkable experience in 1901 by two distinguished scholars, the Principal and Vice-Principal of St Hughes' College, Oxford, when they apparently stepped back in time and witnessed the buildings, gardens and people, including Marie Antoinette, as they would have been prior to the Revolution 112 years before. They published a detailed account of their visit, using pseudonyms, which they called *An Adventure*. Miss Edith Oliver, a former Mayor of Wilton wrote the Preface to the 1931 edition, in which the real names of the authors appeared; she herself experienced somewhat similar visions, including, far out at sea from Land's End, what she afterwards thought must have been a vision of lost Lyonesse.

Miss Oliver was making her first visit to Land's End and on a beautiful bright day she stood on the edge of the cliffs, looking out at the vastness of the sea. As she stared, she saw, to her utter astonishment but with a clarity only dimmed by distance, what appeared to be a town of some importance, seemingly some miles out at sea: a jumble of towers, domes, spires and battlements.

Thinking she must be seeing the Scilly Isles she was still looking at the distant domes and towers when a coastguard approached her. She promptly asked him the name of the town she could see, to which he replied: 'There's no town there; only the sea…' When she looked back, there was no sign of the town she had been looking at for several moments but, when she began to make enquiries, she discovered that others had had a similar experience: seeing, from the precipitous coast of Land's End, what they believed to be part of lost Lyonesse.

A year or two later she had another visionary glimpse of the phantom city. She was driving towards Land's End, accompanied by a friend, Miss MacPherson, one wet and blustery evening, when she again saw those towers and spires and domes, standing immovable far out to sea. 'Do you see anything over there?' she asked her friend. 'Indeed, I do', replied Miss MacPherson, 'I see a city! I've often been told that from here it is possible to catch sight of the lost city of Lyonesse, but I've never seen it before…'

Some years later Miss MacPherson saw the visionary city again when she was accompanied by her sister, who could see nothing.

Stratton

The lands of nearby Binhamy Farm include all that remains of haunted Blanchminster Castle. With the permission of the owner, after crossing a couple of fields, you reach the site of the Crusader, Sir Ranulph de Blanchminster's stronghold.

When he returned from his holy campaign and discovered that his wife had given him up for dead and married another, Sir Ranulph became a recluse. However, as lord of the manor, he was always a great benefactor to Stratton, the small market town mentioned in the Domesday Book that was probably a Roman station. His damaged effigy is to be seen in the fourteenth-century church, but the sad and lonely form of his ghost has also been seen near the still discernible moat of his once-great castle. I talked with a man in 1982 who minutely described the armoured and chain-mailed figure which passed a foot or so above the level of the present ground, until silently, and with an air of inconsolable grief, it melted into nothingness in front of his unbelieving eyes.

Tintagel

Legend has it that King Arthur was conceived and born here, but if he was he had no connection with the present crumbling castle which was not built until six or seven hundred years after his death – but perhaps there was an earlier castle… At all events there have been reported glimpses of the ghostly figure of the great King among these dark ruins and certainly the atmosphere is conducive to such experiences; the aura of mystery which has surrounded Tintagel for centuries has not yet disappeared.

That there is a strange and mystic influence hereabouts is evident from the number of people who believe they have seen or sensed something of the past among these black cliffs and crumbling ruins where, even on the sunniest days, there is a sombre stillness, broken only by the sound of the ever-roaring sea.

Once a year the ruined castle is thought by some people to disappear and re-appear in all its former glory, before returning to its present condition. Barras Head, the headland north of the castle, has a reputation for many strange happenings; dogs in particular often seem to sense something strange and invisible to their human companions. 'There is,' as one resident put it to me, 'something very odd about Barras Head.'

Mrs M King writing from Cranbrook in Kent has told me of a remarkable experience she had when staying near Tintagel.

One night she went to sleep with her bedroom light on and awoke to see a soldier in shining armour standing by her bed. Thinking she must be dreaming, she turned away and put out the bedside light. When she turned back the figure was still there; she put the light on again and found that the figure had disappeared. Next day, a local man told her the house was built on land where battles were fought in King Arthur's time.

Torpoint

Some years ago my friend John Butler, the Baker Street dentist, visited Antony House before it passed into the care of the National Trust. He and a friend were exploring Cornwall, without a map or guide book, going wherever their fancy took them. They came across this impressive house which they began to wander round without a guide, and they started to climb the enormous stairway with its Corinthian columns and bubble lights – blown glass globes of the Queen Anne period. When they were almost at the top of the stairs, facing the green room, John came to a sudden halt and said he could not go on. He saw nothing, but he had the overwhelming impression he was not welcome and should not continue his tour of the house.

Puzzled, for it was a feeling he had never previously experienced, he tried to go on, but the feeling became so strong he turned back, left the house and never did visit the upper rooms.

Years later, John Butler's nurse visited Antony House and in a guide book she discovered that a previous occupant of the house had borne the name Butler!

In 1901 Reginald Carew Pole, aide-de-camp to Lord Roberts in the Afghan War, married Lady Beatrice Butler, daughter of the 3rd Marquess of Ormond. John always wondered whether something had happened at Antony House to someone bearing his name that had left behind an intangible 'something' he had encountered.

Antony House was the scene of a remarkable and well-attested ghost story. In October 1880 Lady Helen Waldegrave visited the Carew Pole family, taking with her her Scottish maid, Helen Alexander, who was taken ill shortly after their arrival. When the local doctor diagnosed typhoid fever one of the housemaids, Frances Reddel, was detailed to serve as night nurse to the ailing girl.

One night the temporary nurse, a very capable and stolid girl, was preparing a dose of medicine when she saw a large, elderly lady enter the bedroom and walk towards the bed. There had been no knock on the door and noticing that the visitor was dressed in a long, red nightgown over a red flannel petticoat (with a hole in it, evidently caused by stay busks!) Frances decided the ill girl's mother must have been sent for. She watched as the figure, carrying an ornate brass candlestick, approached the restive patient, sat on the bed, and looked earnestly at the ill girl. Frances then turned back to her task of preparing the medicine.

A moment later, the medicine ready, she turned and approached the bed to find, to her amazement, that there was no sign of the stout lady she had so plainly seen just seconds earlier! However the condition of the patient soon put all other thoughts out of her mind.

The poor girl was obviously very ill and Frances hurriedly summoned the doctor, but Helen Alexander was beyond human aid and within two hours she was dead.

Two days later the dead girl's family arrived from Scotland and when Frances saw Helen's mother, she almost fainted with shock. In every physical respect this stout, elderly, motherly figure resembled the form she had seen visiting her dying patient two days earlier at four o'clock in the morning. Later, after the funeral, Frances mentioned the incident to Helen's sister who immediately remarked that her mother habitually wore a red nightgown and that she possessed a red flannel petticoat – with a hole in it which the busks of her stays had worn through the material! Furthermore her mother possessed an ornate brass candlestick, such as Frances described.

It was established that neither Helen nor anyone else had written to Helen's parents about the girl being ill, as she was fully convinced she would soon be fit and well again, yet on the evening of her death her mother had suddenly said to her husband: 'I'm worried about Helen. I have a feeling she is very ill...'

No explanation has ever been forthcoming for one of the strangest stories ever to come out of Cornwall, but one possibility is that the figure Frances saw was projected in some way which we do not yet understand from the mind of the dying girl.

Tregeseal

On the outskirts of St Just, Chyoone Farmhouse has been the scene of phantom hoofbeats and the rumble of an unseen coach. Mrs Ethel Waters told Michael Williams she had heard the sounds 'at least a dozen times, maybe twenty times...' They were heard coming down the road, perhaps two or three hundred yards (180-275 metres) away, as if they were turning off the main road, and they always halted at the farm.

One theory to account for the sounds is that a toll house once stood on the site of Chyoone Farmhouse and that the track of the phantom coach and horses follows a turnpike road.

Truro

Here there have been at least two haunted inns. Long ago, a girl was murdered at a hostelry in Castle Street and her form has been glimpsed by sober witnesses, especially in the late evening. The William IV Hotel in Kenwyn Street was reputedly built on the site of a Dominican friary, an oft-repeated snippet of local history that coincides with the ghostly figure of a friar which has been seen hereabouts from time to time.

A field on the outskirts of the town, known as Comprigney, takes its name from the Cornish, 'the field of the gibbet', which it probably once was. There are local people to this day who avoid the area after dark because of 'shadowy figures' that have been seen, and 'rattling chains' that have been heard: visual and audible echoes perhaps from the past...

Veryan

A sixteenth-century house here, once known as Crugsillick Manor, was built by the Kempe family, and it remained in their possession for over three hundred years. One member of the family, Admiral Kempe, a seafarer who had sailed with Captain Cook, seems to return to the house from time to time where he is seen by some people and not others.

In September 1982 I talked with Bill Pilgrim. During the twelve years, prior to 1978, when he and his wife lived at the house, they became completely convinced of the haunting of the place by Admiral Kempe. They never saw anything themselves, but they vouch they were present on each of the four occasions when other people said they saw the figure. None of those who saw the ghost had any knowledge of the place being haunted, of a ghost having been seen there or of anything about Admiral Kempe; yet they all minutely described the same figure. All the four known sightings took place within a period of five years; the figure was always seen in the evening, between seven and nine o'clock, and it always seemed to materialise at the same place on the ground floor and remain within a restricted area. Many other people sensed there was something odd about this part of the house, without actually seeing the ghost or knowing anything about it.

Those who saw the ghost said he had a smile on his face and he certainly never frightened anyone. The general description included grey hair, a long plain coat of some dark material with brass buttons down the front, and strangely square hands. The uniform is thought to be a sort of undress uniform coat worn by officers of the day.

Once, in the middle of the dining room, a guest felt a heavy hand rest on his shoulder and, wondering who it could be, he turned quickly round, to find the dining room deserted. The wife of his friend sitting opposite was even more amazed, for she had seen the ghostly Admiral lay his hand on her friend's shoulder, before vanishing as he turned round.

The house has changed hands many times over the years, each occupant making structural alterations to the place, but the ghost of Admiral Kempe seems to return every so often, irrespective of the environment or the occupants. He has done so for centuries, according to local people who told the Pilgrims, when they asked about any reputed ghost, that the place had been haunted for years by the ghost of the restless Admiral.

Wadebridge

Each New Year's Eve at midnight a phantom coach, drawn by four horses and driven by a headless coachman, is said to gallop through the courtyard of the Molesworth Arms Hotel and out of the hallway… I have been told there are some people who claim to have seen and heard it; others hear it only and see nothing; others again hear and see nothing but feel its presence unmistakably…

The Molesworth Arms in Molesworth Street is one of the old original coaching inns, more than four hundred years old and so named because at one time it was owned by the prominent Molesworth family who were the principal landowners in the area. Today the crest of this distinguished family can still be seen high over the main entrance to the hotel.

Another cyclic ghost is reputed to visit Trewornan Bridge where, once a year, on a night of the full moon a phantom coach and horses races across one of the oldest bridges in Cornwall.

The delightful cottage Treneague beside a little brook known as Hay Stream has long been haunted, in a fittingly quiet and peaceful way, by three ghostly monks. They have been seen sitting on a bench in one of the rooms, drinking ghostly beer. This appearance seems plausible, for the charming house where my wife and I stayed when James and Catherine Turner lived there, is said to have once belonged to the monastery at Pawton, a mile or so away, and to have been one of its out-farms. I found the place utterly peaceful and unhaunted by any troublesome ghost, although I did do an oil painting of the place and included three ghostly monks! And I am sure the present occupants find the atmosphere equally idyllic.

Yet ghosts there are in this part of Cornwall. Listen to Arthur Norway, writing in 1897, for his *Highways and Byways in Devon and Cornwall*: 'This valley of the river Camel is full of haunted lanes and houses. A mile or so up the river stands the ancient church of Egloshayle...here you might see – but never save when the moon is bright – a white rabbit gambolling about the open space beside the churchyard wall; a pretty, long-eared rabbit with pink eyes... it goes loppeting about among the grasses... and if anyone should pass, will sit and look at him with fearless eyes. And well it might. It has nothing to dread from anyone dwelling in these parts...' It seems it is a ghost animal and there are stories of people taking a stick to it in the past, but blows have no effect on ghosts and it was the sticks that were broken, 'as if they had struck a rock'. We are told that no one knows the history of the rabbit, but it has been reported for generations.

There is a story, too, of a man who said he would put an end to the rabbit and he took a gun to it one night. Some of his companions followed at a distance, and soon heard a gun fired and a loud cry... They ran to the place where the ghost rabbit

The former rectory at Warleggan, apparently haunted by the sad figure of the Rev. Frederick Densham

always appeared but neither rabbit nor sportsman was to be seen. At last they found the man, lying dead, with one barrel of his gun discharged and the contents buried in his body. And the ghost of that man may sometimes be seen, leaning over the low wall, pointing a gun at some object which moves quickly in the long grasses...

Warleggan

Even the brilliant sunshine on the day I first visited the former rectory here could not dispel the gloom and apprehension and air of apathy that hung over the place like a heavy cloud of doom. Even the rare optimism and charming company of James and Cathy Turner could not relieve the sense of unhappiness that seemed to hang about this place.

The last incumbent, the eccentric Rev. Frederick William Densham, who served the parish from 1931 to 1953, is thought to still haunt the house and grounds.

The house has a very weird atmosphere; he painted the interior rooms red, yellow and blue – and he painted the interior of the church in the same glaring colours. He built a barbed-wire fence all round the rectory garden, which he guarded with fierce dogs; he refused to hold services at times convenient to his parishioners and generally he lived at odds with the local people. After a church enquiry into his conduct in 1933 the Church Council resigned in a body and never went near the church again. Soon no one went to his services and many entries in the Service Book read on the lines: 'No fog, no wind, no rain, no congregation'. In what surely must have been genuine unhappiness and sorrow he cut out figures in wood and cardboard and fixed them in the pews, and to them he preached and offered Absolution.

He gave the rooms in the rectory Biblical names; he painted large pink crosses on the doors; he preserved an ancient hiding place in the old cellars; and eventually he fell down the stairs and died because he could not reach the bell-pull that would summon his servant who was quartered in the stables.

Long before the Rev. Frederick Densham was here, a previous building that occupied the site was lived in by Ralph de Tremur who is thought to have celebrated Black Mass in the church; certainly he burnt the Host… small wonder that Warleggan is haunted.

When I was there some years ago the house was empty and the garden overgrown. Both are certainly haunted, I was assured, and there are numerous accounts of the sad, dark figure of Frederick Densham walking where he used to walk, towards the empty church, on moonlit nights, or up the drive to the locked and barred door of the empty rectory; sitting where he used to sit and preaching where he used to preach in his torn cassock and dusty hat.

I heard stories of many odd happenings, some possibly paranormal in origin and of the strange individuals who are drawn to Warleggan, but they never seem to stay very long in this place of ghosts and hollow memories.

Wendron

A few years ago my wife and I sought out Bodilly Farm, reputedly the scene of a curious manifestation which, perhaps even more curiously, has never been followed up and thoroughly

A miner and his family at Wendron in the mid-nineteenth century

investigated. We saw the place where treasure may still be hidden but the occupants at that time were not prepared to co-operate in any practical investigation of the intriguing story. The case came to my knowledge through my good friend Air Commodore R Carter Jonas who had come across the story as a boy and had been puzzled and baffled by the tale ever since.

The story goes, according to a one-time Methodist minister of Goldsithney near Penzance, that many years ago a miner sought to rent a house he liked at Wendron, but he discovered the place was reputed to be haunted and indeed the owner was reluctant to let the place because so many people had taken it but never stayed long... However the miner ridiculed the idea of ghosts, and he and his mother and sister were soon established in the house.

Even at that time it was a quaint old place with only two rooms downstairs, but tremendous rooms they were, like great barns. At one end of the room used as a kitchen there was a wide, old-fashioned open fireplace, large enough to seat several people.

A few days after moving into the place the miner was out at work when his mother, sitting at the 'fringle' fire, heard the latch of the door lifted. She looked round and saw, to her surprise, the door open and what looked like a black calf walk in, look round and walk out again, the door latching itself behind it! Thinking she must have been dreaming, she made no mention of the matter when her son returned home later in the day; but from that time onwards weird noises repeatedly disturbed the family at night when they were in bed. The miner did his utmost to fathom the mysterious sounds, searching every corner and crevice of the house, but he failed to find any clue or explanation.

Then one night the miner's mother was awakened by the sound of someone in her room and striking a light she was astonished to see three diminutive figures standing in a row beside her bed. She hastily blew out the light and hid among the bedclothes until she heard the figures depart. When she peeped out of the bedclothes there was no sign of the strange little people she had seen.

A few nights later the performance was repeated and when it happened a third time the old lady plucked up sufficient courage to enquire what her visitors wanted. One of the unbidden guests immediately replied: 'You are the first who has ever spoken to us and we have come to do you good'.

He then told her to break down the plaster between two windows in her son's bedroom and she would find a place like a chimney. At the bottom of the chimney she should dig until she reached a large stone. Beneath that stone she would find 'abundant wealth for herself and her family'.

So certain was the old lady that this had been no dream and so impressed was she by the earnestness and sincerity of her visitors she lost no time in relating everything that had happened to her son and daughter, who in turn consulted a second son who lived a few miles away. He, too, was impressed by the story and they all decided to test its accuracy by breaking into the plaster at the spot that had been indicated.

That night they tore down the plaster between the two windows which stood in the north wall, and there, sure enough, was a large aperture, exactly as though a chimney had been pierced, although no fireplace existed and the clean state of the stonework suggested there had never been a fireplace there. By means of a strong rope the miner was lowered into the aperture which he discovered led like a secret passage to the ground, where it ended.

Having proved the story to be true so far the excited family soon set to work and shifted an enormous amount of earth and rubble until eventually a huge flat stone or boulder was exposed. It was concluded this must be the stone that had been referred to. The miner tried working round the stone but soon realised blasting would be necessary to remove the boulder and settle the mystery once and for all. A hole was bored ready for the charge and then it was decided to wait until the following night.

Sadly the next day the miner met with a terrible accident in the mine where he was employed: both his hands were blown off at the wrists and he was almost scalped. When he was carried home his mother prepared a bed for him in the kitchen.

Next day the bedroom was cleared as much as possible, a sheet was tucked up to cover the mouth of the shaft, and the mutilated miner was carried upstairs to his own bedroom. Several of his fellow miners offered to take turns to sit up with their comrade at night and some, more curious than the others, lifted the sheet, discovered the hole and the rumour began to circulate in the immediate area that the injured miner had found a rich lode and was mining on his own account.

After several days, hovering between this world and the next, the miner died and after the funeral, fearing the consequences now that their labours had been discovered, the miner's brother threw as much rubble as he could lay his hands on back into the

Bodilly Farm at Wendron, where there may be both ghosts and hidden treasure awaiting discovery

hole and replastered the wall. So, for the time being, the adventure ended and soon afterwards the old lady and her daughter moved to live with a relative some miles away.

Years later the old lady's grandson, who had heard the story as a boy, enlisted the help of a miner friend and set out to seek for the quaint house and searched for the treasure. They found the old house had been pulled down and a new and substantial farmhouse built in its place.

Their enquiries resulted in the owner allowing them to excavate on the land to see whether they could locate the old shaft. Meanwhile they sought out a former owner who remembered the rumour that the place had been mined and said: 'Perhaps you know that the large slab of slate on which the fire is usually built in the 'fringle' opens upon a flight of steps?'

After the old lady and her daughter left the house a couple moved in and accidentally discovered the flight of steps, obtained a lantern and hurriedly went down to explore. They said they found a large room filled with armour, swords and bronze articles. As they were exploring the place their lantern was suddenly blown out and, thinking they were in a room occupied by ghosts, they hastily rushed up the steps, slammed down the slab of slate to cover the entrance and never told anyone what they had done until the old house had been pulled down and another built in its place.

The listening miners realised that in all probability the lamp had been extinguished by foul air and they were more convinced than ever that the treasure was there for the finding.

After a lot of hard work they located the foundations of the old house and, working round them, were delighted when they hit upon the old shaft, but it ran beneath the existing house. They eagerly sought permission to burrow further in search of the old cellars, but the owner became frightened lest the building should be undermined and collapse, and nothing would induce him to consent to them delving and excavating underneath his house.

There are stories of the old house being a smugglers' hide-out and the practice of burying treasure was by no means uncommon in smuggling days. So there may still be a fortune waiting for someone who is adventurous enough to seek for treasure that seems to have been revealed by ghostly visitors.

When visiting Bodilly Farm in 1959 a prominent Ghost Club Society investigator was told that the shaft had been filled in. When I was there more than thirty years later I was shown a concrete cattle-yard which had, I was told, been built over the shaft. Perhaps some competent metal detector or diviner could locate the exact whereabouts of whatever still lies buried at Bodilly Farm. It seems such a pity not to verify or disprove a long-standing mystery.

Select Bibliography

Alexander, Marc, *Ghostly Cornwall* (Pacific Press, 1977)
   Haunted Churches and Abbeys of Britain (Arthur Barker, 1978)
   Haunted Inns (Frederick Muller, 1973)
   Phantom Britain (Frederick Muller, 1975)
Braddock, Joseph, *Haunted Houses* (Batsford, 1956)
Brown, Raymond Lamont, *Phantoms, Legends, Customs and
   Superstitions of the Sea* (Patrick Stephens, 1972)
Coxe, Antony D. Hippisley, *Haunted Britain* (Hutchinson, 1973)
du Maurier, Daphne, *Vanishing Cornwall* (Victor Gollancz, 1967)
Deane, Tony, and Shaw, Tony, *The Folklore of Cornwall* (Batsford,
   1975)
Francis, Di, *Cornish Ghosts* (James Pike, 1977)
Green, Andrew, *Ghosts of Today* (Kaye & Ward, 1980)
   Our Haunted Kingdom (Wolfe, 1973)
Hallam, Jack, *The Ghosts' Who's Who* (David & Charles, 1977)
Hunt, Robert, *Popular Romances of the West of England* (Chatto &
   Windus, 1871)
Kenward, Trevor, and Snow, Robert, *Pengersick Castle*, 1977
   (Kenward, 26 Dewlands Road, Verwood, Dorset BH31 6PL)
Moss, Peter, *Ghosts over Britain* (Elm Tree Books, 1977)
Norman, Diana, *The Stately Ghosts of England* (Frederick Muller,
   1963)
Norway, Arthur H, *Highways and Byways in Devon and Cornwall*
   (Macmillan, 1897)
Smit, Tim, *The Lost Gardens of Heligan* (Gollancz, 1997)
Turner, James, *Ghosts in the South West* (David and Charles, 1973)
Underwood, Peter, *A Host of Hauntings* (Leslie Frewin, 1973)
   Gazetteer of British Ghosts (Souvenir Press, 1971)
   Ghostly encounters South-west (Bossiney Books, 2002)
   This Haunted Isle (Eric Dobby, 1993)
   Guide to Ghosts and Haunted Places (Piatkus, 1996)
   West Country Hauntings (Bossiney Books, 2002)
Williams, Michael, *Ghost hunting South-west* (Bossiney Books, 2003)
   Ghosts around Bodmin Moor (Bossiney Books, 2005)

More Ghostly manifestations from Bossiney Books...

Ghost-hunting South-West
Michael Williams

Ghosts around Bodmin Moor
Michael Williams

Ghosts of Devon
Peter Underwood

Ghosts of Dorset
Peter Underwood

Ghosts of North Devon
Peter Underwood

Ghosts of Somerset
Peter Underwood

Ghostly encounters
Peter Underwood

Supernatural Dartmoor
Michael Williams

West Country Hauntings
Peter Underwood